EMBRACING

Grace

EMBRACING
Grace

RECONCILING RELATIONSHIPS WITH PEOPLE AND GOD

JUDY BAKER

HENSLEY
PUBLISHING

TULSA, OKLAHOMA

HENSLEY
PUBLISHING

ISBN 1-56322-083-0

Embracing Grace

To my husband, Bruce —

God used you to teach me

how to be a team player.

Thank you for your love

and support.

I love you.

ABOUT PHOTOCOPYING

CONTENTS

INTRODUCTION

All this is from God, who reconciled us to himself through Christ and gave us the ministry of reconciliation.

2 Corinthians 5:18

Reconciliation is important to God! In fact, our Father puts such importance on reconciliation that He sacrificed His only Son so that we could be reconciled to Him and have eternal life. Father God also calls every believer to the ministry of reconciliation. It is not a special gift or an option. It is a command and a calling to all believers without exception. And because God equips us for everything He calls us to, we each have the ability to forgive others, reconcile our relationships, and extend God's love and grace. It is a matter of surrendering our will to His, abandoning our own self-interest and agendas for the interests of the Holy Spirit, and seeing everything through God's eyes so that His will becomes our motivation. The most important questions in your life become: "How will this affect my Lord?" and "What would bring glory to Jesus Christ?" Does this lifestyle sound impossible? Luke 1:37 tells us, *With God nothing shall be impossible.* (KJV)

Several years ago, I began to fervently pray, *God, I want to know You. I want You to remove all of me and replace it with all of You.* That request was the first step on my walk down the road of reconciliation. This journey has confirmed for me the validity of Hebrews 12:11: *No discipline seems pleasant at the time, but painful. Later on, however, it produces a harvest of righteousness and peace for those who have been trained by it.* Let me assure you that the fruit of righteousness and peace is well worth the effort it takes to walk the road of reconciliation!

Over the next nine weeks, we will explore what the Word of God has to say about reconciliation. We will discover what it means to our walk with the Lord and how we relate to fellow believers, as well as its potential impact on the unsaved. So, my friend, please join me as we seek the heart of *Jehovah-M'Kaddesh,* The Lord who Sanctifies.

Week 1

RECONCILIATION: THE DEFINITION

Welcome to the first week of our study on reconciliation – a ministry to which we are all called. We will begin our study by defining reconciliation, including our need to be reconciled to God and the provision which makes that possible. Through God's Word, we will learn how the enemy creates division; the weapons we will use to defeat him; how to release bitterness by being rooted in the fruit of the Spirit; and the definitions of sin and grace. It is my prayer that through this study you will come to know the Lord in new, more intimate ways as you follow Him in His ministry of reconciliation.

DAY 1
A Minister? Who, Me?

DAY 2
Opposites Don't Always Attract

DAY 3
The Apple of His Eye

DAY 4
What Kind of Seeds Are You Planting?

DAY 5
A Team Player

A MINISTER? WHO, ME?

God made him who had no sin to be sin for us, so that in him we might become the righteousness of God.

2 Corinthians 5:21

We are the "They" who have been called to reach out! God calls all Christians to the ministry of reconciliation, and we are all to be active members of the body of Christ in truth, love, and grace.

The need for reconciliation is crucial – it touches every aspect of our lives and the lives of those around us. In our society today, we have an epidemic of broken relationships. Marriages and families are in crisis. More important, our spiritual lives are in crisis. We go to church on Sunday mornings to get our "warm fuzzies," then complain that some unnamed "They" are not reaching out to us. The truth is, *we are the "They" who have been called to reach out!* God calls all Christians to the ministry of reconciliation, and we are all to be active members of the body of Christ in truth, love, and grace.

Unfortunately, many of us are consumed with the unfairness in our lives. Our conversations focus on ourselves – how something affects "me" or "my needs," and what "they" should do to fix it. Bookstores, magazine shelves, and talk shows are filled with selfish solutions, so-called "expert" opinions on how to rectify these situations.

The Bible is the place to find truth and guidance for every issue in our lives. For true healing to take place in the depth of our hearts, God must be involved.

The truth is, the Bible is the place to find truth and guidance for every issue in our lives. For true healing to take place in the depth of our hearts, God must be involved. Otherwise, we are just temporarily solving a few issues in our own ability, and the results will not stand. But when reconciliation is based on God's power and character rather than on "me," "my" ability, and "my" circumstances, His healing will sustain us year after year.

I spent most of my life trying to fix myself and everyone around me. If I couldn't immediately come up with a workable solution on my own, a few hours on the telephone with my friends usually resulted in a new and improved plan. Whenever I had a problem or a joy, I would reach for the phone to call someone – my husband or a friend – for comfort, for advice, or to share my happiness. Only when they could not help me, did I turn to God.

God had to bring me to a place where I trusted Him and called on Him first in crisis or in joy. Two years after my husband and I built our "dream home," God called us to move to another city. We sold our home and moved from the Houston suburb where we had lived for fourteen years to a small town where we knew no one.

Separated from all my friends and everything familiar, I learned to turn to God first, then my husband and friends. It wasn't easy. Many times, during this period of isolation, I would find myself reaching for the phone and hearing that still, small voice calling me to Him first. What freedom I received the day I finally placed the need to do things my own way on the altar and left it there!

I have learned that when I allow God to be in charge, less "reconciling" is usually needed in my relationships!

Isaiah 55:9 tells me that God's ways and thoughts are always higher (and better) than mine. I have learned that when I allow God to be in charge, less "reconciling" is usually needed in my relationships! God is the planner, the reconciler. He works through you and me to touch those around us, and we can trust His leading and guidance.

Read Matthew 7:24-29.

Who is the ultimate authority in your life? *Mainly I Run to the Father, but sometimes I look to Rich or others.*

When everything crashes around you, to whom do you first turn for comfort? *Same as above*

To understand God's Word, we need to look at Scripture in context. Sometimes that means we must determine the meaning of the original Greek or Hebrew words. These languages are much more precise and descriptive than English, and when studied, the true and deeper meaning of the passage becomes clear. In this study we will pull the scriptures apart and look at their original meanings to better understand God's purpose.

Read the following scripture passage, noting the following definitions of the emphasized words.

> *All this is from God, who reconciled us to himself through Christ and* ***gave*** *us the ministry of* ***reconciliation:*** *that God was reconciling the world to himself in Christ, not counting men's sins against them. And he has* ***committed*** *to us the* ***message*** *of reconciliation. We are therefore Christ's ambassadors, as though God were making his* ***appeal*** *through us. We implore you on Christ's behalf: Be reconciled to God. God* ***made*** *him who had no sin to be sin for us, so that in him we might become the* ***righteousness*** *of God.*
>
> *2 Corinthians 5:18-21*

Gave: "Commissioned and supplied"
Reconciliation: "An exchange for others or a return to favor"
Committed: "Ordained or established"
Message: "A spoken word"
Appeal: "A call to one's side or an exhortation"

Made: "Acted rightly, done by God before any action on our part"
Righteousness: "Integrity, virtue, or correctness of thinking"

God sent His Son to

return us to favor with

the Father and to die for

our sins so we could

have eternal life.

God sent His Son to return us to favor with the Father and to die for our sins so we could have eternal life. After we were reconciled to God, He commissioned us to become ministers of reconciliation. But He didn't send us out alone. The Greek word translated *gave* in verse 18 is *didomi* meaning to supply or to furnish necessary things.[1] God promises that He will supply us with what we need for this ministry.

Can you think of a time when God led you to do a task for which you felt totally inadequate? *Yes, when Pastor Micah asked for me to direct Sunday Lighthouse.*

How did He equip you to accomplish this mission? *By giving me people to fill in where positions needed to be filled as well as help where needed.*

Do you realize that God has ordained us as His ministers of reconciliation to each other and to a lost and dying world? We are His instruments to show Jesus to other believers and to the unsaved. What an incredible privilege and awesome responsibility! It might be totally overwhelming if we had to do it on our own. But God told us that He will supply us with everything we need for the task.

Referring back to the previous definitions, write 2 Corinthians 5:21 in your own words. *Jesus chose to take my place on the cross, who was sinless, paid for my guilt, shame, & sin, so I could be made holy in the sight of my heavenly Father & forgiven.*

Through Jesus' suffering,

we are completely

forgiven by our Father.

Jesus Christ is the Passover Lamb sent by our Father to totally pay for our sins. The perfect, unblemished Lamb of God took our past, present, and future sins as if they were His own. He fully experienced the pain, guilt, and shame of our sins – to the same depth of intimate familiarity as that shared in the sexual union of a husband and wife. We became one with Him at Calvary, and He paid the price for our sins. Through Jesus' suffering, we are completely forgiven by our Father, and when we accept Jesus Christ as our Lord and Savior, that forgiveness brings about our reconciliation to God. Christ's righteousness, integrity, and purity of thought and deed become ours as well.

Beloved, this is amazing grace! The Father's incredible love for you makes your reconciliation possible. Take a few moments to ponder the incredible debt canceled by the heavenly Father who sacrificed His Son – His only Son, whom He loved –

for you. You are so precious to God that even if you were the only person on earth in need of salvation, Jesus would have died just for you.

The Father's incredible love for you makes your reconciliation possible.

Read 1 John 4:10 and 1 Peter 2:4-10. Write out a prayer of praise and thanksgiving to your heavenly Father.

_____

_____

_____

_____

_____

Read Acts 26:17-18 and consider the following thoughts.

In his book *My Utmost for His Highest*, Oswald Chambers wrote:

> This verse is the greatest example of the true essence of a disciple of Jesus Christ in all of the New Testament. God's first sovereign work of grace is summed up in the words "that they may receive the forgiveness of sins." This is followed by God's second mighty work of grace. In sanctification, the one who has been born again deliberately gives up his right to himself to Jesus Christ, and identifies Himself entirely with God's ministry to others.[2]

In Acts 26:17-18, Jesus ordained Paul for ministry. Because we are also ordained for ministry, we can look to these verses and define the ministry of reconciliation as follows:

Reconciliation: Jesus died for our sins and restores us to God when we accept the free gift of His salvation.

Sanctification: When we give up our rights to ourselves and allow God to take control, we become reconciled to His likeness, which in turn draws others to Him. Christ in us draws them to His grace, and we become His representatives to a lost and hurting world. However, even though we have the authority to represent Him, only God Himself is the healer of hurts and strongholds.

Galatians 2:20-21 says:

> *I have been crucified with Christ and I no longer live, but Christ lives in me. The life I live in the body, I live by faith in the Son of God, who loved me and gave himself for me. I do not set aside the grace of God, for if righteousness could be gained through the law, Christ died for nothing.*

Many people accept Jesus Christ only as Savior, not as Lord. They want the basic "fire insurance" of eternal life, but nothing more. Paul understood that God has called us to make Jesus both our Savior and Lord. When we accept Jesus, we

Paul understood that God has called us to make Jesus both our Savior and Lord.

become a new creation in Christ, with the Holy Spirit residing within us. As Christians, we crucify our old sin nature on the cross of Christ. Because Jesus is now both our Savior and Lord, our lives change. Our sanctification puts God in control of our lives, our thoughts, and our desires, as we respond to His amazing love for us. We put Him first, above everything and everyone.

Read 1 John 3:19-21, Jeremiah 17:9, and Hebrews 12:11.

Is there something in your life that you hold more precious than God? What do you need to do to give up your rights to yourself and let God take control? Ask God to reveal to you what areas of your life are more dear to you than Him. According to 1 John 3:20, God can change your heart, if you give it to Him. Ask Him to change your desires until they conform to His desires. By allowing God to discipline your heart, you will experience the fruit of righteousness and peace that only comes from above.

TRUTHS TO EMBRACE

_____

_____

_____

_____

_____

_____

OPPOSITES DON'T ALWAYS ATTRACT

From the lips of children and infants you have ordained praise because of your enemies, to silence the foe and the avenger.

Psalm 8:2

The opposite of reconciliation is division. As Christians, we are called to minister reconciliation. The world ministers division; its goal is to prevent any reconciliation from taking place. We are involved in spiritual warfare, and Satan, the prince of this world, wants to separate us from God and each other. Satan understands the divide-and-conquer principle.

Why do we Christians sometimes take the ostrich approach to spiritual warfare? Do we "stick our heads in the sand" because talking about evil makes us uncomfortable or seems controversial to our man-made church doctrines?

In this study, we will look only to God's Word for our instruction and allow God to show us His truth. Satan tries to cause division in the following areas of our lives:

- Our reconciliation to God
- Our reconciliation in relationships with one another
- Our witness to unbelievers, which reconciles them to God

Satan loves to divide Christians from each other and from God, because such divisions prevent us from living victorious lives and take our focus off the Lord. Division stems from the bitter roots of jealousy, hatred, and unforgiveness which grow, spread, and kill like cancer. But unlike cancer, a divisive attitude is contagious; it steals joy and peace, silences our praise, destroys families, and is passed from generation to generation.

The divinely inspired Word of God gives us instruction on how to confront division. When the Bible says something, we must trust and believe it, especially in this potentially destructive area. The Scriptures teach us that the spirit of division must be dealt with through spiritual warfare. Let's look at what the Bible has to say about spiritual warfare.

Read Psalm 86 and answer the following questions.

As Christians, we are called to minister reconciliation.

Verse 2	Who is able to guard your life? _____
Verse 4	Who brings you joy?_____
Verse 7	On whom are you to call in times of trouble? _____
Verse 8	Who is so wonderful that none can compare to Him? _____
Verse 9	Whom are you to worship and glorify? _____
Verse 11	Who gives you an *undivided heart* when you learn His ways and walk in His truth? _____
Verse 12	Whom are you to praise with all your heart? _____
Verse 13	Whose great love for you delivered you from the depths of the grave? _____

Read Psalm 30 and answer the following questions.

Verse 1	Whom are you to exalt because He lifted you out of the depths?_____
Verse 2	When you call for help, who will heal you? _____
Verse 3	Who spared you from going down into the pit? _____
Verse 4	To whom are you to sing, and whose holy name are you to praise? ____
Verse 11	Who turns your wailing into dancing, removes your sackcloth, and clothes you with joy? _____

According to verse 12, when you focus on praising God with an undivided heart, what will be the uncontrollable natural response? _____
_____
_____
_____
_____

According to Isaiah 43:20-21, why were you created? _____
_____
_____

Read Psalm 8:2, then fill in the blanks below.

From the lips of children and infants you have _____ *praise because of your enemies, to* _____ *the foe and the* _____ .

The Hebrew root word for the word translated here as *foe* means someone who binds, ties up, and causes distress or presses hard upon.[3] The root word for *avenger* means someone who has revengeful feelings.[4]

According to Ephesians 4:31, whom do some of the foes and avengers in our lives include? _____
_____

What area in your life has you bound up or is pressing hard on you, keeping you from praising God? _____

_____

In the *King James Version*, the word *strength* is used instead of *praise*. The Hebrew word for *strength* is *oze*, which means strength in praise, power, and might.[5] God demands our praises because He knows that when we praise Him, our focus is on Him and not on ourselves. Praise brings us to the very throne room of God and puts us in harmony and agreement with Him. This is when we receive the strength and power to fight Satan, the instigator of division – when we focus on Father God, there is no room for division among us.

Read Psalm 8:2 again. What weapon with divine power has the Father given you?

_____

In the summer of 1998, I began having hormone problems, which caused me to fall into a pit of deep depression. For six months, everything in my life became distorted. My thought processes were confused. I was physically exhausted. My emotions were completely off balance. I was a perfect target for the enemy because he preys on the weak and lonely. I pulled away from everything and everyone as I continued to spiral downward. I even pulled away from church as the enemy used my depression to create division. At this lowest point of my life, I could not pray, I could not get out of bed, I could not even talk to my husband or best friend. During that time Jesus became my best friend, because I did not have to explain anything to Him or even speak in His presence. In that dark period, Jesus just loved and held me. I cherished that relationship; it made no demands when I had nothing to give.

The enemy loves to wreak havoc in our minds and then have us replay the tapes repeatedly. Maybe we have a heated discussion or argument with someone – we play it in our heads over and over again. We struggle with guilt or imagine what we "should" have said, and this can drive us to *deep depression!*

Many days I literally held my hands on the sides of my face and said, "Don't think, don't think, don't think," because I realized how distorted my thought processes were, and I wanted to stop the monotonous replays.

Later, when I got a little stronger, I again held my hands on the sides of my face, this time saying, "Focus on the Lord, focus on the Lord, focus on the Lord." At that point, my mind was just grabbing on to the Lord to keep from totally drowning. I sat in silence most of the time, even without any music. I would praise God out of obedience in prayer, but not in song. God eventually healed me enough that I could listen to worship music again. But I still could not sing. As time progressed, I was finally able to praise Him in song again. That is when the healing power went into

Praise brings us to the very throne room of God and puts us in harmony and agreement with Him.

The enemy loves to wreak havoc in our minds and then have us replay the tapes repeatedly.

overdrive. Throughout those six months of severe depression, I tried desperately to stay focused on the Lord, but praise was the weapon that kept Satan from causing a total division in my life with my Lord, my friends, and my church. Beloved, I know the weapon of praise worked a mighty miracle in my life and the life of my church family, because 1 John 4:4 tells me *"greater is he that is in you, than he that is in the world."* (KJV)

> *May our dependably steady and warmly personal God develop maturity in you so that you get along with each other as well as Jesus gets along with us all. Then we'll be a choir — not our voices only, but our very lives singing in harmony in a stunning anthem to the God and Father of our Master Jesus!*
>
> Romans 15:5-6 THE MESSAGE

What is your focus? When you are still, are the tapes of division playing continually in your mind? I urge you to place those tapes on the altar and leave them there. Then place your hands on your face and say, "Focus on God, focus on God." Keep praise music playing in your home and your car. God inhabits the praises of His people, and Satan cannot stay when the Lord is praised. Fight spiritual warfare with the mighty weapon of praise.

TRUTHS TO EMBRACE

_____

_____

_____

_____

_____

_____

Week One, Day Three

THE APPLE OF HIS EYE

Love the Lord your God with all your heart and with all your soul and with all your mind and with all your strength.

Mark 12:30

Very often God brings us to the point where we have to decide what is most important to us — Him or something else.

Read Genesis 15:1-5. Write down Abraham's desire and God's promise. _____
_____
_____

Read Genesis 21:1-5. After waiting many years for God's promise to be fulfilled, how old was Abraham when Isaac was born? _____

Abraham spent most of his life childless, yet he believed God's promise that one day his seed would be the means through which God's covenant would be fulfilled. Knowing this, how do you think Abraham felt toward Isaac? _____
_____

By all accounts, Isaac was special to his dad. He may have been spoiled, coddled, and treated like a prince. He was a very long-awaited baby and the beginning of God's fulfillment of the covenant with Abraham to make his descendants as numerous as the dust on the earth.

My husband loves all of our four children equally. First, the Lord gave us three wonderful sons. Then, He added our daughter, Beth. We lovingly call her the "little princess," because on the day she was born her daddy placed her on a throne. She is very precious to him, and he would protect her at all costs. This long-awaited daughter will always have a special place in her daddy's heart. She is the apple of his eye.

According to Zechariah 2:8 and Deuteronomy 32:10, how does Father God describe His children?

_____

Very often God brings us to the point where we have to decide what is most important to us — Him or something else.

How does Proverbs 7:2 tell us we are to view the importance of keeping God's commandments? _____

_____

_____

In Psalm 17:8, David was seeking protection. How did he describe the relationship he desired with his heavenly Father? _____

_____

In Hebrew, the "apple of the eye" refers to the pupil, the center part of the eye which focuses the vision of the person.

The phrase "apple of the eye" originated from the Hebrew language. In Hebrew, the "apple of the eye" refers to the pupil, the center part of the eye which focuses the vision of the person. It is the critical part of the eye that must be protected at all cost – without the pupil we cannot see. God positioned the pupil in the skull in such a way that it is protected.

Similarly, because Beth is the apple of her daddy's eye, he would do whatever it took within his human limitations to protect her. But even more important, Beth is the apple of her heavenly Father's eye. And His ability to protect her is limitless. God's love for Beth is infinitely greater than Bruce's capability to love her.

Read Genesis 22:1-18. What was Abraham asked to place on the altar of sacrifice?

_____

Why do you think God asked him to make such a sacrifice? _____

_____

In Genesis 22:2, we see the first time in Scripture that God uses the word *love*:

> Then God said, "Take your son, your only son, Isaac, whom you love,
> and go to the region of Moriah. Sacrifice him there as a burnt offering on
> one of the mountains I will tell you about."

Father God desires that you love Him first, and then your spouse, your children, your friends, and your career.

Mark 12:30 tells us Jesus said that the first and most important commandment was to *Love the Lord your God with all your* _____ *and with all your* _____ *and with all your* _____ *and with all your* _____.

Father God desires that you love Him *first,* and then your spouse, your children, your friends, and your career. Nothing is ever to supersede your love for your Father. In fact, that is so imperative that many times in Scripture the Word commands you to love, seek, turn, rejoice, and serve Him with all your heart. God desires and commands your heart first and completely. He, in return, loves you and protects you at all costs. He was even willing to sacrifice His Son, His only Son whom He loves, in order to protect you from eternal damnation. It cost God everything He held dear, but you are worth it because you are the apple of His eye.

What comparison can you make between Genesis 22:2 and Mark 12:30? _____
_____
_____

Father God placed His most precious, beloved, only Son on the altar of sacrifice for our sins in order to reconcile us to Him.

Father God placed His most precious, beloved, only Son on the altar of sacrifice for our sins in order to reconcile us to Him. Through Abraham and Isaac's experience on Mount Moriah, God gave us a picture of Jesus' future sacrifice as well as the sacrifice that would be required of us. Many times the "precious loves" of our lives – like our families – seem harmless and good, but if we are putting them above God, they can still keep us out of God's will.

Read Hebrews 12:15 below:

> *See to it that no one misses the grace of God and that no bitter root grows up to cause trouble and defile many.*

A few months ago, a girlfriend and I went on a "girls-only" vacation. Each day we got up early to participate in various activities, and we were looking forward to the last day, when we had planned to sleep late. Unfortunately, her husband called at 7 o'clock that morning, just to say hello! I am not a morning person. When I answered the phone and discovered who it was and why he'd called, I was livid. All I could think was how inconsiderate he had been to wake us up on our vacation. In fact, I was so upset that I couldn't go back to sleep. Then, I heard that still, small voice telling me, "Judy, unforgiveness hurts you more than the person you won't forgive. He has gone on to work, happy after talking to his wife. You can't go back to sleep because of your anger and unforgiveness. Get over it! Forgive him and go back to sleep!"

Father God does not ask us to forgive because He wants to make things difficult for us; He asks us to forgive because unforgiveness puts us in bondage.

On a more serious note, a very dear woman in my life is a Christian who has allowed bitterness to consume her. Like most sins, her bitterness started out small but grew. By her own admission, she has never been able to forgive and forget. But not only does she not forgive, she talks about the hurts and disappointments over and over again to anyone who will listen. Through the years, this unforgiveness has grown into a deep and binding bitterness which, like a cancer, has spread to divide and destroy her family. It has so consumed her that it has now made her who she is – a bitter, old woman.

Father God does not ask us to forgive because He wants to make things difficult for us; He asks us to forgive because unforgiveness puts *us* in bondage.

That's why Paul wrote in Ephesians 3:17-18: *I pray that you, being rooted and established in love, may have power, together with all the saints, to grasp how wide and long and high and deep is the love of Christ.* Only then will we be free of the bondage of sin and be filled with good fruit.

Look up the following scripture references, then write them in the chart next to the trait they denote.

Romans 8:1	James 4:11-12	Galatians 5:18-21
Romans 15:5	Colossians 2:8	2 Timothy 3:16-17
Romans 8:37-39	Colossians 1:21-22	Galatians 5:22-23
Job 4:4	Hebrews 10:24	Ephesians 5:4 and 4:29
2 Corinthians 4:13-15	Matthew 10:19-20	1 Corinthians 6:7
2 Peter 2:18-22	1 Peter 5:8	Matthew 12:32

Traits of the Tender Shoot Traits of the Bitter Root

	Tender Shoot		Bitter Root
	No condemnation		Judgment and slander
	Victory ("conquers all")		Defeat ("devours")
	Unity		Division
	Grace		Hurtful sarcasm
	God-given words		Condemning words
	Freedom from accusation		False promises
	God-breathed Scripture		Deceptive philosophy, human traditions, and legalism
	Encouragement		Discouragement
	Fruit of the Spirit		Bitter fruit

Write out Hebrews 12:14-15.

_____

_____

_____

_____

Whatever we are "rooted in" is what others will see.

Beloved, do you see how important it is to be rooted and grounded in the love of Jesus? We are our Father's world. Our lives, our words, and our actions are to be a witness of Jesus and His love. Whatever we are "rooted in" is what others will see. If, in your heart, you are rooted in anger, jealousy, unforgiveness, or criticism, your life will show evidence of the root of bitterness.

Two dear Christian women, sisters, were sexually abused by their father. After much counseling and prayer, the older sister was able to forgive her father and reconcile with him before his death. She is a pleasure to be around because of the peace and joy in her life that come only from the Lord. Since her deliverance from this bondage, her marriage has become stronger, as have her relationships with her children. Although the younger sister is also a Christian, she has never allowed the Lord to heal this part of her life. She would tell you that she hates her dad, but the past does not bother her. Yet, she is consumed with bitterness from her anger and unforgiveness. In fact, she asks that since life is miserable, why shouldn't she be as well? She is always badgering her non-Christian husband about not going to church. But he questions why he should want to be a Christian, like her, when she is constantly miserable. He is missing the grace of God because of the root of bitterness in his wife's life.

Beloved, do you see how important it is that we are rooted and grounded in the love of Jesus? We are our Father's ministers of reconciliation to the body of Christ and to a lost world. Our lives, our words, and our actions are to be a witness of Jesus and His love. Whatever we are "rooted in" is what others will see. If, in your heart, you are rooted in anger, jealousy, unforgiveness, or criticism, your life will show evidence of the root of bitterness.

We are our Father's ministers of reconciliation to the body of Christ and to a lost world.

We Christians need to live with a godly love for all those around us. First Peter 4:8 tells us that *love covers a multitude of sins.* We must exhibit something different in all circumstances, something which will draw others to Jesus. That something different – not eloquent words, not being able to quote scripture, not knocking on doors with the Roman Road to Salvation – is what brings about reconciliation. In Galatians 5:22-23 Paul wrote: *The fruit of the Spirit is love, joy, peace, patience, kindness, goodness, faithfulness, gentleness, and self-control.* This is the difference we must exhibit through our lives in all circumstances.

We Christians need to live with a godly love for all those around us.

Several years ago, my husband's cousins were visiting us. Marsha and Tom are not Christians. One morning Marsha looked at me and asked, "What is it that's different about you? With all the turmoil in your life, how do you manage to stay calm and go forward with such joy?" I replied that my life was based on the Lord Jesus Christ and not my circumstances; that what she saw was the Holy Spirit within me; and that I didn't think that I could even get up in the morning without the Lord.

Always be aware that the world is watching. Do they see holiness in your life, or bitterness? Pray 1 Peter 1:13-16 and ask the Lord to show you any root of bitterness in your heart. As Abraham did, place it on the altar of sacrifice, and then let the Lord replace it with His love and grace.

TRUTHS TO EMBRACE

_____

_____

_____

_____

_____

_____

WHAT KIND OF SEEDS ARE YOU PLANTING?

You have been born again, not of perishable seed, but of imperishable, through the living and enduring word of God.

1 Peter 1:23

"Sin splatters." That's what my friend, Miki, says. A quick glance at our society confirms her observation.

The world tells us our first concern should be ourselves. Take for example, abortion. Pro-choice supporters believe the decision to terminate a pregnancy is solely the mother's, because the pregnancy affects her body. The reality is, her decision affects not just her life but the lives of the baby, the father, the grandparents, and her future husband and children.

That's why the friends we associate with, the movies, television programs, music, and books we take in are all so important. In fact, every aspect of your life affects other people in one way or another. They all affect the way we think, speak, and act.

We are constantly producing fruit for the world around us. Some of this fruit is healthy, brings healing, and glorifies God; however, much of our fruit has a bitter taste.

Read John 15:16-17. What do you consider lasting fruit? _____
_____
_____
_____

We should act, think, and talk the same way on Sunday morning as we do Saturday night or Monday morning.

The things we say and do send a clear message to those around us. We can tell our children to do as we say and not as we do, but the message they will hear is told by our actions — not our empty words. We should act, think, and talk the same way on Sunday morning as we do Saturday night or Monday morning. Anything less sends the message that we don't really believe what we say and do at church; it is just an act.

Read John 17:18-23. Why did Jesus consider our life message important? _____
_____
_____

UNREALISTIC EXPECTATIONS

I have always set very high goals and expectations for my life. Unfortunately, I also inadvertently set those same high goals and standards for those around me. This is legalism, and it is a sin of which I have had to repent more than once. I wrapped my expectations of others in a neat little package saying, "I just want the best for them," or "I just want them to treat me like I treat them." And when they didn't return the favor, I was hurt. Poor me!

The problem with this way of thinking is that it revolves around "me" — my standards, my hopes, my rules, and my self-righteousness. Does that sound like anyone you've read about? Perhaps the Pharisees in Jesus' day?

When our expectations differ from reality, the result is often anger. What other emotions might we experience? _____
_____
_____

When reality fails to measure up to our expectations, we can experience not only anger, but also feelings of division, apathy, rejection, insecurity, unforgiveness, and depression. Unfortunately, all of these feelings provide fertile soil in which bitterness can take root.

Can you think of situations in which you have placed unrealistic expectations on yourself or others, expectations that left you feeling angry when they were not met?
_____
_____

Unrealistic expectations are the seeds of legalism that we plant instead of God's seeds of grace.

Unrealistic expectations are the seeds of legalism that we plant instead of God's seeds of grace. Legalism says, "You are:
- unworthy."
- not good enough."
- not meeting the standard."
- needing to work harder."
- loved conditionally."
- accepted conditionally."

Grace, however, says the opposite. Grace extends love and acceptance *unconditionally*.

Read Galatians 5:7-10 and John 15:16-17, and fill in the following blanks.

_____ sows to please his sinful nature. The seeds of legalism will not last. _____ sows to please the Spirit. The seeds of grace will last.

God has given me the gift of discernment. When I am depending on the Spirit, I can walk into a situation, assess it, and form a plan. Often, I discern things about people. However, when I am depending on myself, this gift of discernment turns into a critical spirit. The difference in the seeds that I plant with this gift is determined by what I do with the information. Am I critical, or do I go to the throne of grace in prayer for that person or situation?

What does Matthew 7:1-5 say about judging? _____
_____

There is no gray area here. We are not to judge other people. Legalists criticize in self-righteousness, thinking they are not as bad as those they judge. However, as Christians, our standard is not other people – our standard is the Lord Jesus Christ.

When we measure our goodness against His, we can only feel shame for our inadequacies. That's why it is very important that God and His Word must always be our standard.

As Christians, our standard is not other people – our standard is the Lord Jesus Christ.

Read Colossians 2:8 and fill in the following blanks with the correct word.

See to it that no one takes you _____ through hollow and deceptive philosophy, which depends on human _____ and the basic principles of this _____ rather than on _____.

The Greek word translated *deceptive* in this verse is *kenos*. It means used of men, destitute of spiritual wealth, and fruitless.[6] Legalism is a hollow and deceptive philosophy that depends on human tradition and the basic principles of the world. We must also test the catchy little phrases we Christians use to be certain they are true to God's Word.

Based on 1 John 5:1, how would you define sin?_____
_____

Our focus is always to be on the Lord and His glory. When I am focused on God and not myself, the effects of sin in my life are secondary.

Our focus is always to be on the Lord and His glory. When I am focused on God and not myself, the effects of sin in my life are secondary. First John 5:3 says, *This is love for God: to obey his commands.* When I break His commands, it shows my lack of love for Him and that I love my flesh nature more than God. Sin clearly shows the ways in which I don't love God. This changes everything about the way we view reconciliation and our spiritual walk.

Sin may splatter, but blessings also spill over to those around us. Because the Father has called all believers to reconciliation, I want to plant spiritual seeds that draw people to Him. I want people to see the Holy Spirit in my life. I do not want to be judgmental or critical. I put my legalism on the altar and replace it with the grace of God.

Praise and worship of my Lord is a passion of mine. I still have much to learn, but God has been teaching me lately about the importance of praise. Praising God has become a major part of my day. My time alone with God to praise Him is the best for me, but very often corporate "praise and worship" has been a disappointment to me. Issues in my own life and limitations the church body places on me has caused some of this disappointment. Everyone likes different styles of music, and I think the music minister often receives too many "helpful suggestions" from the congregation. Personally, I prefer contemporary music but the bottom line is that it really doesn't matter what I prefer because praise is for God. When we come in honest and open worship and praise of our holy God, our focus is on Him and His glory. As a result of loving the Father this way, we reap the fruit of joy. And that fruit will be evident to others.

One day when I was a senior in high school, I was singing at home, and my mother mentioned that I was off key. Not being one who takes criticism easily, I was embarrassed, and I quit singing altogether. From that moment on, I believed I could not sing. I began to mouth the words in church, or arrive after the music was finished. At ladies' retreats, there was always lots of music, but I would literally get physically sick and stay in the bathroom until it was over. I loved music and I loved to sing, but I was embarrassed to do it around anyone else. This was a sin, because I was more concerned with what others thought than what God thought! I would sing if I were alone in my car or in the shower and I could turn the volume up so loud that even I could not hear my voice. For many years I prayed for God to heal me. But to add insult to injury, God brought a very precious friend into my life who had an absolutely beautiful voice. Now the problem escalated to the point of not just feeling inferior, but having my throat just close up in fear to the point that I couldn't even make a sound. This would happen in groups or when I was alone – it didn't seem to matter.

One day after my prayer time, God revealed that I needed to ask my friend to help me learn to sing. I thought, *You have got to be kidding, Lord! This is embarrassing enough, but she sounds so great, and I sound so bad!* For several weeks I tried to ignore God's direction. Finally, one night we were driving back from my son's college swim meet and I could no longer ignore the Lord's request. I tried to explain to her what I needed, but I got so upset I had to pull off the road. She was so excited when I asked her to help me sing. But I got even more upset because she tried to make me

When we come in honest and open worship and praise of our holy God, our focus is on Him and His glory.

sing with her right there in the car. God had obviously posted a sentry of angels around the car, because I don't know how we made it home. Finally, I just drove silently as God began to convict me of my sin.

When we arrived at my house, I asked her to come in and pray with me. I knelt to pray and something amazing happened. I could not utter a word verbally or even in my mind. I was consumed with shame for the way that I hadn't been loving my God in praise and worship. It was one of the darkest moments of my life, because I felt so separated from Him. At this point, it didn't matter exactly what my sin was – it just mattered that I had not loved and honored my Father as He had asked. In addition, this was during a time when I had been actively praying for God to replace our minister of music; I felt that our services were too dry and that he had been performance-driven rather than in tune with the heart of God. Besides not honoring God with my own songs, I was guilty of hypocrisy and legalism – I was committing the same sin that I had been pointing out in someone else. My "performance" for God and those around me when I sang was more important to me than pleasing my Father. Knowing that I couldn't give a perfect performance, I didn't even try.

God commands our praises, not talented performances. I should be willing to make that "joyful noise," because if I am truly praising God, it will be as if only He and I are in the room. When I go to His throne of grace, it shouldn't matter what others think, because my praise is for Him alone. I wish I could tell you that this happened not long after I was saved, while I was still a baby Christian. But the truth is that I have known the Lord most of my life, walked closely with Him for many years, and was in church leadership and teaching a Bible study at the time.

If I am truly praising God, it will be as if only He and I are in the room.

Legalism comes in all kinds of packages, in all walks of our Christian life. We never *arrive!* I never understood shame before that night. I had been sorry for my sin and had tried to repent, but I realized that until you truly experience shame, you never really understand what it means to be saved by grace. Shame illuminates the fact that there is nothing good in us save Christ Jesus. Shame takes our pride and places it at the foot of the cross, where it belongs. When we give God our pride and our self-righteousness, we are no longer able to criticize others; instead, we discern their sin and hurts and extend God's love and grace to them, unconditionally and without judgment. We will intercede in love for them, because we know, in our hearts, that "there, except by the grace of God, go I." In our depravity, we are capable of doing just what they are doing, or worse!

After what seemed an eternity, my Lord took my shame, just as He had done on the cross at Calvary, and the darkness lifted. I rested in His arms and experienced a love and comfort that words could never express. I was covered in His grace. My friend went to bed, but I could not leave His presence in that room. I praised Him until dawn, when He gave me this word.

I will exalt you, O LORD, for you lifted me out of the depths and did not let my enemies gloat over me. O LORD my God, I called to you for help and you healed me.

O LORD, you brought me up from the grave; you spared me from going down into the pit. Sing to the LORD, you saints of his; praise his holy name. For his anger lasts only a moment, but his favor lasts a lifetime; weeping may remain for a night, but rejoicing comes in the morning.

When I felt secure, I said, "I will never be shaken." O LORD, when you favored me, you made my mountain stand firm; but when you hid your face, I was dismayed.

To you, O LORD, I called; to the LORD I cried for mercy: "What gain is there in my destruction, in my going down into the pit? Will the dust praise you? Will it proclaim your faithfulness? Hear, O LORD, and be merciful to me; O LORD, be my help."

You turned my wailing into dancing; you removed my sackcloth and clothed me with joy, that my heart may sing to you and not be silent. O LORD my God, I will give you thanks forever.

Psalm 30:1-12

Ask **Jehovah M'Kaddesh**, the Lord who Sanctifies, to begin to reveal the legalism in your life and to prepare your heart so that you will truly experience shame for your sins. Ask Him to show you the ways that you don't love Him enough, so that you may repent. Then He will turn your wailing into dancing and remove your sackcloth so that you will be clothed in joy. Write your prayer in the space below.

TRUTHS TO EMBRACE

_____

_____

_____

_____

_____

_____

Week One, Day Five

A TEAM PLAYER

The body is a unit, though it is made up of many parts; and though all its parts are many, they form one body. So it is with Christ.

1 Corinthians 12:12

My husband, Bruce, is a natural athlete. Besides enjoying sports in general, he was an all-star baseball and basketball player who went to college on a full scholarship. During his formative years, Bruce learned the value of being a team player and respecting the coach as the decision-maker. He knows that winning is a team effort. Bruce brought these values into our marriage and into his business. He has taught our family that we must work together (and often make sacrifices) for the good of the group.

In order for the body of Christ to function as God intended, Christians must also have a team mentality. We must recognize that it takes the combined efforts of people – in the forefront, in the background, on the sidelines, and in the stands – to succeed.

In order for the body of Christ to function as God intended, Christians must also have a team mentality.

Read 1 Corinthians 12:12-20. Why do you think God calls us to be team players?

_____

_____

Read Numbers 32:1-32 and answer the following questions.

What did the Gadites and Reubenites ask of Moses? _____

_____

Why didn't they want to settle in the Promised Land? _____

_____

_____

What was Moses' response? Why? _____

_____

_____

What did Moses require of them if he granted their request? _____

_____

_____

Who decided to join them in settling outside of the Promised Land? _____
_____
_____

Why do you think they did that? _____
_____

As we learned yesterday, our choices affect those around us. The Gadites and Reubenites saw a land that looked good and decided to settle there instead of waiting to see what God had in store for them in the Promised Land. In doing what they wanted instead of what God told them to do, they settled for less than God's best, because they didn't want to leave their comfort zone.

We are often the same way.

At one time, Bruce and I belonged to a church that experienced an amazing move of God. Walls came down, families were reconciled, and healing occurred among the body. But a group within the fellowship grew upset and resisted, saying, "This is not the way we've always done things." They were unwilling to give up control, and as a result, the church went back to the status quo.

Why did these people risk everything to follow God? Because they were willing to leave their comfort zones for God's greatest glory and the advancement of His kingdom on earth.

When we look at the lives of biblical characters, we will not find one to whom God said, "You're doing great! Stay just the way you are." The men and women found in Scripture had to leave their comfort zones. Abraham left his home to go to an unknown land. Jonah went to Nineveh to preach to people he didn't even like. Mary risked death by conceiving a child before marriage. The disciples left their homes and families to follow Christ.

Why did these people risk everything to follow God? Because they were willing to leave their comfort zones for God's greatest glory and the advancement of His kingdom on earth.

In our earlier look at Numbers, we saw that when Moses granted the Reubenites and the Gadites permission to settle outside the Promised Land, half of the tribe of Manasseh decided to join them.

Now read 2 Kings 10:32-33. Who were the first tribes to fall into captivity?
_____
_____

Why do you think God allowed them to be first?
_____

How often we drag others down with us!

For four years, I resisted God's calling to surrender my life to ministry. Because I was in my forties, I reasoned that I was too old. Even more of a factor was that I was embarrassed that it had taken forty years for me to come to the place that He called others to as teenagers. This, coupled with the facts that my family required a lot of my time, and that I lacked the education and talent that I thought were prerequisites to being in the ministry, hindered me from laying it all down. Yet, before and during this time, I prayed saying, *Whatever, Lord* – but all the while thinking that He surely couldn't mean this!

One day after Bible study, as I knelt at the altar to pray, God again called me to surrender my life to ministry. This time there was no more reasoning or discussion. I simply said, *Yes, Lord, whatever You want. I don't understand why, how, or where, but it no longer matters. I love You, trust You, and will follow You anywhere.* Had I continued to ignore God's call, I would have settled for less than His best. I have no idea where He will lead, but wherever He goes, I want to follow.

Read Acts 4:13. What were Peter and John's qualifications to be on God's reconciliation team? _____

_____

_____

_____

To be a team player, we must trust God.

To be a team player, we must trust God.

The Greek word translated *submission* is *hypotasso*. It is a military term meaning to arrange troop divisions in a military fashion under the command of a leader. In non-military use, it is a voluntary attitude of giving in, cooperating, assuming responsibility, and carrying a burden.[7]

Over the years, I have told my children countless times that when I tell them to do something, they need to trust me and "do it now." I cannot always explain the reason for my instructions, but some day their lives may depend on following my directions.

Submitting to authority is a place of great safety.

Submitting to authority is a place of great safety. The same principle holds true in our spiritual lives. We are called to submit to our leaders unless they ask us to do something contrary to God's Word. We must submit even when we don't understand, or when we disagree. When I submit to my husband, pastor, or others in authority over me, then I honor God's command and can trust Him to handle the decision-makers if they are wrong. Otherwise, He will deal with my insubordination first.

Read 1 Peter 1:13-25 and answer the following questions.

Why are we to submit? _____

_____

What is the kingdom outcome of our submission? _____

_____

Do you consider Jesus submissive? Why? _____

_____

According to Ephesians 5:21-24, how are we to submit? _____

_____

What does Proverbs 21:1 say about God's ability to handle kings and officials?

_____

Do you think this refers to pagan kings only? Why? _____

_____

_____

Read Matthew 26:36-50.

What did Jesus desire? _____

_____

What was the Father's will? _____

_____

Why do you think Jesus was willing to put His desires aside to do His Father's will?

_____

_____

_____

When was the last time your desire was in conflict with what you knew to be your heavenly Father's will? What was the outcome? _____

_____

_____

Read Acts 20:22-24. Why was Paul going to Jerusalem? _____

_____

Do you consider Paul a team player? Why? _____
_____

The Greek word translated in verse 22 as *bound* or *compelled* is *deo*, meaning to bind, to tie, or to fasten.[8] Paul understood that believers are guided by the Holy Spirit every minute of the day because they are literally bound together. Jesus said that nothing can remove us from His hand. We are His children. We are on His team today, tomorrow, and forever. We can choose to be in the starting line-up, or we can ignore the coach and always be late to practice. We must choose wisely since we are representatives of God's team to a lost world.

God has an unbeatable game plan. All we have to do is get out of the way and follow His lead.

God has an unbeatable game plan. All we have to do is get out of the way and follow His lead. When it comes to the end of my life, I want to be able to say like Paul:

> *For I am already being poured out like a drink offering, and the time has come for my departure. I have fought the good fight, I have finished the race, I have kept the faith. Now there is in store for me the crown of righteousness, which the Lord, the righteous Judge, will award to me on that day—and not only to me, but also to all who have longed for his appearing.*
>
> *2 Timothy 4:6-8*

Spend some time meditating on today's lesson and ask God to reveal to you the areas of your life that are keeping you from running the race and completing the tasks He has given you. Place this willfulness at His feet and ask Him to bring your desires in line with His will. Write out your prayer in the space below.

TRUTHS TO EMBRACE

_____
_____
_____
_____
_____
_____

Week 2

THE WEAPON OF FORGIVENESS

This week we will explore forgiveness. We will search the scriptures to find out why God tells us to forgive. We will discover that forgiving someone does not necessarily mean that they were right and we were wrong. We will also learn that our focus determines our reality. When we think of forgiveness, we usually picture ourselves forgiving others, but it is also important to face our pride honestly so that we can forgive God and ourselves as well. When we don't forgive, the results can be deadly. Praise God that He has given us the weapon of forgiveness. With this weapon, we can gain the victory with the Lord on our side.

DAY 1
Not Fair!

DAY 2
What's Your Focus?

DAY 3
Me First

DAY 4
Adonai

DAY 5
Stressed Out!

NOT FAIR!

What is more, I consider everything a loss compared to the surpassing greatness of knowing Christ Jesus my Lord, for whose sake I have lost all things.

Philippians 3:8

One of the biggest stumbling blocks to forgiveness is our thinking that to forgive someone means to say that they were right and we were wrong. Not so! Father God forgives us, and He is perfect, holy, and righteous.

Read Luke 23:20-34.

What crime had Jesus committed? _____

_____

What did He ask of the Father? Why? _____

_____

Jesus was deity living as a man. He experienced all of the emotional hurt and pain that we feel.

Do you think this request came easily? Why? _____

_____

Read Ephesians 4:31-5:2.

Write out Ephesians 5:1 in the space given. _____

_____

God wants to remove our heavy packs of unforgiveness and bitterness so that we can kneel before Him in reverence and then stand up in freedom.

The Lord understands your hurts and pains. He knows how costly it is to forgive someone who has done something horrible to you. He considers your forgiveness a fragrant sacrifice to a holy God who loves you more than you can fathom.

In Luke 18:23-25, Jesus mentioned the "eye of the needle." During this period of history, cities were encompassed by walls that were designed to protect inhabitants from attack. At dawn, the main gates were opened for all to pass through. At sunset, however, the gates were closed for protection and no one was allowed through. At night, a small door in the wall next to the gate was used for emergencies. This opening, called the "eye of the needle," was only large enough for one man to pass through. If a camel needed to go through this door, all of its packs were removed, so it could kneel down, bow its head, and crawl through. In a similar manner, God wants to remove our heavy packs of unforgiveness and bitterness so that we can kneel before Him in reverence and then stand up in freedom.

Read Hebrews 11:8-16. According to these verses, where is our home? _____
_____
_____

My husband and I recently put our house on the market. It is a beautiful home in which I have felt very blessed to live. However, we believe the Lord is moving our lives in a different direction. Buying a home usually signifies that you're settling in and putting down roots, and its furnishings reveal a lot about you, as well as your priorities and values.

When you claim ownership of your hurts, when you settle into them and allow them to take root, you make them your home. And in the same way a house reflects the personality of its owners, these hurts become your identity. It is easy to become so wrapped up in your hurts that you are more at home with them than you are with God's peace.

My son Carl has a seizure disorder. His seizures are mild, lasting only for thirty to sixty seconds. Unfortunately, he is not allowed to drive since he cannot risk being unconscious for even a few seconds. Other than not driving, the seizures have little effect on his life. However, not driving is horrendous to a teenage boy, and Carl has had to deal with a lot of anger regarding his disorder. Certainly, the seizures are not his fault, nor did he do anything to deserve them. His anger is understandable, and yet God calls Carl to let it go because the truth is, his anger hurts him more than the offense of the illness.

WHERE ARE YOU MAKING YOUR HOME?

Read John 11:1-37; 12:1-8.

How would you describe Mary? _____
_____
_____

What was her relationship to Jesus? _____
_____
_____

What did Judas recommend be done with the perfume? _____
_____
_____

How did Jesus respond to his suggestion? _____
_____
_____

> *For God is greater than our hearts, and he knows everything. Dear friends, if our hearts do not condemn us, we have confidence before God and receive from him anything we ask, because we obey his commands and do what pleases him. And this is his command: to believe in the name of his Son, Jesus Christ, and to love one another as he commanded us. Those who obey his commands live in him, and he in them. And this is how we know that he lives in us: We know it by the Spirit he gave us.*
>
> *1 John 3:20-24*

What is your bottle of nard? What are you holding on to because it hurts too much and the cost seems too great to let it go? Ask the Lord to give you the desire to release it. I myself have very strong hands so I often hold on to physical things very tightly. Often I pray for God to pry spiritual or emotional issues literally out of my hands if necessary, because in my heart I want to give these things to Him.

TRUTHS TO EMBRACE

_____
_____
_____
_____
_____
_____

WHAT'S YOUR FOCUS?

And whatever you do, whether in word or deed, do it all in the name of the Lord Jesus, giving thanks to God the Father through him.

Colossians 3:17

"Your focus determines your reality."

I am not a big movie fan. Much of the material that comes out of Hollywood offends me, so I try to guard what I put in my mind. However, my family loves *Star Wars*, so seeing it was a must. As we sat through the movie, we came to the scene where a Jedi knight tells young Anakin Skywalker to focus, because "your focus determines your reality." What a truth!

Read Luke 4:18-21. What is our reality in Christ? _____
_____
_____

When we focus on ourselves, our reality is self-righteousness and self-centeredness. When we focus on our circumstances, our reality can become hopelessness and depression. But when we focus on the Lord, our reality is hope, joy, and peace in the midst of circumstances.

Read Ephesians 4:32 and Colossians 3:13. What does God's Word command us to do? _____
_____
_____

According to Matthew 18:21-22, is there a limit on how many times we have to forgive someone? Why? _____
_____
_____

According to Luke 8:21, if we hear God's Word and put it into practice, what kind of person are we? _____
_____
_____

When your focus is on the Lord, how should this change your response to those who offend you? _____
_____

Read Genesis 37.

How did Joseph's brothers feel about him? _____

_____

_____

How do you think Joseph felt knowing that his brothers were united in hating him?

_____

_____

Have you ever felt like the outcast in your family, church, neighborhood, or workplace?_____

_____

If you answered "yes," what emotions did you feel? How did you handle those feelings? _____

_____

_____

Does it still bother you? Where was your focus? _____

_____

_____

Go back to Genesis 37 and re-read verse 22.

What did Joseph's brothers plan to do to him? _____

_____

_____

_____

How did their original plan change? Why? _____

_____

_____

How do you think this made Joseph feel? _____

_____

_____

For what did his brothers sell Joseph? _____

How old was Joseph when this happened?_____

Read Genesis 39.

How does this passage describe Joseph? _____

_____

Why did he refuse to have an affair with Potiphar's wife? _____

_____

_____

_____

Complete the following verse from Genesis 39:10: *And though she spoke to Joseph day after day, he refused to go to bed with her or* _____

_____

_____ .

This is where Joseph's character is truly revealed. He understood that flirting with sin was just one step away from committing the sin. Joseph had the "right" to complain about being thrown in prison, but he didn't! He kept his integrity, even there.

It is not a sin to have hurts, but what we do with our hurts can become a sin.

When we share our hurts with others in hopes they will validate our right to be hurt, we are flirting with sin. It is not a sin to have hurts, but what we do with our hurts can become a sin. God calls us to forgive those who have offended us — not allow hurt feelings to become the sin of unforgiveness.

Read Genesis 40. How did the cupbearer repay Joseph for his insight and encouragement? _____

_____

_____

Two years passed before the cupbearer remembered his promise to Joseph. Joseph was brought to Pharaoh to interpret a dream that no one in all of Egypt could decipher. The Lord spoke to Pharaoh through Joseph.

According to Genesis 41:37-40, how did Pharaoh respond? _____

_____

_____

By now Joseph was thirty years old. While in Pharaoh's service, he had married and had two sons.

What did he name them and why? _____

_____

_____

_____

Isn't it amazing that when you forgive, God makes you fruitful in your painful situation? More important, He is glorified. Joseph became a minister of reconciliation in a pagan nation. His focus on God was steadfast, even in the midst of painful circumstances, and his focus determined his reality. As a result, he was able to help an entire nation and was reunited with his family.

Read Colossians 3:13-17. Stay focused, O beloved child of God, for your focus determines your reality.

TRUTHS TO EMBRACE

_____
_____
_____
_____
_____
_____

Week Two, Day Three

ME FIRST

I will set out and go back to my father and say to him: Father, I have sinned against heaven and against you.

Luke 15:18

"Getting real" in the body of Christ starts with an honest look inside. Basically, all sin stems from the sin of pride. In Genesis 3, Eve thought she knew better than God and that with more knowledge, she could be like Him. You and I are no different.

Some of us can extend grace and forgiveness to everyone but ourselves. Like the older brother in the parable of the prodigal son, we have not grasped the truth, and we think more highly of ourselves than we should. We think we should be above doing certain things because we have arrived at a higher spiritual plane than others. The reality is that we never arrive. We only become more accountable for the knowledge that God has imparted to us. Hopefully, we will someday reach a point where we respond rather than react. We must always keep our focus on the Lord and know that without His grace, we are capable of anything.

Others of us, like the prodigal son, think that our past sins are too grievous to be forgiven. But this is equivalent to thumbing your nose at God's grace. It is saying that His grace can cover some things, but Jesus' sacrificial death on the cross was not enough for what you did. Wrong!

Read Luke 15:11-32. Are you more like the elder brother or the prodigal son? Why?

_____

_____

_____

In 1 Corinthians 15:7-10, what does Paul teach us about the grace of God? _____

_____

_____

The Message Bible says:

> *He then spent time with James and the rest of those He commissioned to represent him; and then He finally presented Himself alive to me. It was fitting that I bring up the rear. I don't deserve to be included in that inner circle, as you well know, having spent all those early years trying my best*

Some of us can extend grace and forgiveness to everyone but ourselves.

Others of us, like the prodigal son, think that our past sins are too grievous to be forgiven.

to stamp God's church right out of existence. But because God was so gracious, so very generous, here I am. And I'm not about to let his grace go to waste. Haven't I worked hard trying to do more than any of the others? Even then, my work didn't amount to all that much. It was God giving me the work to do, God giving me the energy to do it.

1 Corinthians 15:7-10 THE MESSAGE

Grace was precious to Paul because he had experienced it in the depth of his soul. He knew firsthand how hard it was to be good enough.

Paul, more than any other apostle, taught God's grace. Grace was precious to Paul because he had experienced it in the depth of his soul. He knew firsthand how hard it was to be good enough. That is why Paul wrote:

It is we who are the circumcision, we who worship by the Spirit of God, who glory in Christ Jesus, and who put no confidence in the flesh— though I myself have reasons for such confidence. If anyone else thinks he has reasons to put confidence in the flesh, I have more: circumcised on the eighth day, of the people of Israel, of the tribe of Benjamin, a Hebrew of Hebrews; in regard to the law, a Pharisee; as for zeal, persecuting the church; as for legalistic righteousness, faultless. But whatever was to my profit I now consider loss for the sake of Christ.

Philippians 3:3-7

Paul did all the right things with a zeal for God, yet in his vigor he missed God altogether. Have you ever been there? I know I have. Because of my pride, I have trouble forgiving myself. It pains me that I cannot be good enough to not sin. I want to control my emotions, actions, and words instead of accepting that there is nothing good in me except Jesus Christ and His righteousness. It is called being *legalistic.* We are the elder brothers: the ones who have been in church all our lives, always follow the rules, and do the right thing. It sounds pretty noble, but the legalists are also the control freaks, the writers and enforcers of the church rules. They are the ones who carry the *Robert's Rules of Church Service* in their purse or back pocket. They think they are above these so-called "big" sins – like sexual immorality, adultery, or murder. Now don't get offended. The reason I know about these traits is because, like Paul, this was me.

It was very hard for me to forgive myself because I kept thinking that I should know better. I didn't want anyone to know my sins because that would ruin my image. I could understand someone else stumbling, but I worked too hard to have stumbled myself. In principle, I wanted to accept God's grace. But in reality, I wanted to be good enough that I really didn't need it. PRIDE, PRIDE, PRIDE!!!

Write out Proverbs 11:2. _____

_____

Paul also understood what it was to commit a sin so grievous that it would seem too great to forgive.

According to Acts 9:1-2 and Acts 26:9-11, what mission was Paul pursuing?

_____

_____

Continue reading Acts 9:3-19 and Acts 26:12-18.

What did the Lord do to Saul? _____

_____

_____

According to Jesus, whom was Saul persecuting? _____

_____

_____

Sin is the ways we don't love God.

This is a perfect example of focus. From a human standpoint, it seemed as though Saul was only hurting the people he persecuted. But from a godly focus, Saul was persecuting the Lord. Remember our definition of sin: *Sin is the ways we don't love God.* Saul would need to ask God's forgiveness first, then forgive himself, and then ask forgiveness of those he persecuted. How do you forgive yourself for killing innocent people? There is no way you can make amends. The repercussions of that sin are irrevocable.

What was wrong with Saul when he stood up? _____

_____

After Ananias prayed for Saul, what happened? _____

_____

STRONGHOLDS

I once had a teacher who defined a stronghold as "a way of thinking through which everything we see or hear is filtered and therefore comes out distorted and bent." She compared it to looking through glasses with red lenses. She said, "I could tell you all day that the sky is blue, but if you are looking through those red lenses, the sky looks red to you. Nothing I say or do can convince you otherwise, because you are seeing red."

When a sin takes root in our life, it becomes a stronghold. Everything we say, do, or hear is filtered through that stronghold.

When a sin takes root in our life, it becomes a stronghold. Everything we say, do, or hear is filtered through that stronghold. That is why it is so important that we repent of sin. Saul fell to the ground a sinful unbeliever. He stood up a sinner saved by grace just like you and me. When the scales (the red lenses) fell from Saul's eyes, he saw things clearly for the first time because he saw them through God's eyes.

Why do you think God uses sinful people like Paul? _____
_____

No amount of good works could ever change the facts. Paul was simply saved by the grace of God.

If He can use Paul, can He use you or me? Why? _____
_____

I think God sent Paul to witness to the Gentiles because he now understood how they would feel. To the Jews, the Gentiles were unworthy simply because of their birthright. There was nothing they could ever do to be good enough to be a Jew. Paul understood Jewish law. He also now understood that all of his good works were worthless. He was the lowest of sinners – he had persecuted and killed Christians. Nothing could ever make up for that. No amount of good works could ever change the facts. Paul was simply saved by the grace of God. God could use Paul because he no longer had the wrong perception. Paul knew who he was apart from the grace of God, and he knew exactly what he was capable of without God's grace. He now had two options: He could dwell on the past, believing that what he had done was too awful to forgive, and attempt to make up for his sin with more good works, *or* he could be honest about his sins, accept God's forgiveness, and forgive himself, then press on to the goal to which God was calling him. Paul chose to let God work through him to witness to the Gentiles.

Read Acts 28:31 and fill in the blanks below.

> *Boldly and without* _____ *he preached the kingdom of God and* _____ *about the Lord Jesus Christ.*

What does Acts 19:11 say about how God was able to use Paul? _____
_____

How does 1 Corinthians 1:26-2:5 apply to your life? _____
_____

Ask God to search your heart to reveal what is hindering you from being used in extraordinary ways. Remember, it is God's ability and your availability. Forgive yourself today.

TRUTHS TO EMBRACE

_____

_____

_____

_____

_____

_____

_____

_____

ADONAI

You will seek me and find me when you seek me with all your heart.

Jeremiah 29:13

Joseph was able to forgive his brothers because he was in a right relationship with his Lord.

Have you ever prayed, *I want to be just like You, Jesus?* I have. Of course, in my immaturity what I meant was that I wanted to be gentle, loving, wise, and discerning – in other words, a really nice person who was very spiritual and helped others.

Yes, those are all wonderful qualities of Jesus, but I really didn't consider what was involved in being *like* Jesus. Well, if you ever prayed as I did only to get a different answer than you expected, don't feel bad because you are in good company. James and John thought the same way.

What did Jesus mean in Matthew 20:22? _____

_____

To be like Jesus means to walk the road of suffering – being unjustly accused, persecuted, and spat upon. Many people believe the Christian life is problem-free; however, their beliefs are not in line with the life of Jesus. The Word of God *never* says our lives will be carefree and easy.

Look up the following scriptures and fill in the blanks.

For it has been granted to you on behalf of Christ not only to believe on him, but also to _____ for him.

Philippians 1:29

In this you greatly rejoice, though now for a little while you may have had to _____ grief in all kinds of trials. These have come so that your faith—of greater worth than gold, which perishes even though refined by fire—may be proved genuine and may result in praise, glory and honor when Jesus Christ is revealed. Though you have not seen him, you love him; and even though you do not see him now, you believe in him and are filled with an inexpressible and glorious joy, for you are receiving the goal of your faith, the salvation of your souls.

1 Peter 1:6-9

But how is it to your credit if you receive a beating for doing wrong and endure it? But if you _____ for doing good and you endure it, this is commendable before God. To this you were called, because Christ suffered for you, leaving you an example, that you should follow in his steps.

1 Peter 2:20-21

However, if you _____ as a Christian, do not be ashamed, but praise God that you bear that name.

1 Peter 4:16

So then, those who _____ according to God's will should commit themselves to their faithful Creator and continue to do good.

1 Peter 4:19

How would you summarize the above verses and apply them to your life? _____
_____
_____

Joseph lived a peaceful life for a while. He was his father's favorite son and as a result, he received preferential treatment, especially the coat of many colors. One day Joseph's brothers decided they had had enough of Joseph's special treatment, so they sold him into slavery and told their father that a wild animal had killed him. Joseph spent the next thirteen years in slavery and in prison before becoming second in command only to Pharaoh.

Read Genesis 45:1-15.

When Joseph was reunited with his brothers, how did he respond to them? _____
_____
_____

How do you think he was able to do this? _____
_____
_____
_____

Have you ever been wronged by someone and then come face to face with that person years later? What was your response? How did it make you feel? How did you feel toward God for allowing this to happen to you? _____
_____
_____

After Joseph's father died, his brothers worried that Joseph would seek revenge against them. They were expecting him to react to them in the same way they would have.

Read Genesis 50:15-21, and write out Joseph's response to his brothers._____
_____
_____

One of the things I love about studying the Bible is how it fits together perfectly. The Old and New Testament are not autonomous books. God's truths are the same both before and after Jesus' time on earth.

When we approach the throne of grace, God promises us that we will find grace to help us in our time of need.

Read Romans 8:28 and explain how it applies to Joseph's situation. _____
_____
_____
_____
_____

Joseph was able to forgive his brothers because he was in a right relationship with his Lord. He could have blamed both his brothers and God for the direction of his life. From a human standpoint, he had plenty to complain about. "Why me?" he could have said. "What did I do to deserve this? I was a good son. I served God. I didn't sleep with Potiphar's wife, even though I could have, and most men would have! This is just not fair. I'm here in prison in a foreign country, and my brothers, who betrayed me, are at home with Dad, dividing up my inheritance. THIS IS NOT FAIR, GOD! WHY ARE YOU LETTING THIS HAPPEN TO ME?"

Have you ever felt this way? _____
_____
_____
_____
_____

It's okay to tell God – He knows it anyway! He's a big God, and He's not going to fall off the throne just because you are upset with Him. He is your heavenly Father, your *Abba*.

Write out Hebrews 4:16. _____
_____
_____
_____

The Greek word translated here as *boldly* or *confidence* is *parrhesia*. It means freedom in speaking, unreservedness in speech, free and fearless confidence or speaking openly, frankly, and without concealment.[1] To come to the throne of grace with confidence is to march into the throne room and come nose to nose with your heavenly Daddy. You can talk to Him with fearless freedom and confidence, openly and frankly. There is absolutely nothing that you cannot talk to Him about. Nothing you say or do will change His love for you because His love is never based on your performance. It is always based on His character and on the Lord Jesus Christ.

Things always seem better after you talk them out. You are not the first person to get mad at God. But you do need to come to a place where you repent of your expectations of God's fixing your life for you just the way you want. You need to forgive Him for allowing persecution in your life.

When you *approach the throne of grace with confidence, so that you may receive mercy and find grace to help you in your time of need,* you will find that your perception will change. When you come with confidence into the throne room, what you will discover there is the heart of God.

When we approach the throne of grace, God promises us that we will *find* grace to help us in our time of need. The Greek word translated *find* is *heurisko*. It means after searching to find a thing sought, to return to a place, to discover or understand, to get knowledge of God, or to come to know God.[2] When we come with confidence into the throne room, we discover God's heart towards us.

The following passage from Joel 2:18-19 further reveals God's heart for His children:

> *Then the LORD will be jealous for His land and take pity on His people.*
> *The LORD will reply to them: "I am sending you grain, new wine and oil,*
> *enough to satisfy you fully; never again will I make you an object of scorn*
> *to the nations."*

The word *jealous* is used eight times in the Old Testament. In the Hebrew it is defined as the attributes of God's justice and holiness as He is the sole object of human worship and does not tolerate man's sins.[3] Beloved, God is jealous for you. He wants the best for His children. This is why He wants you to give Him your unforgiveness; He knows the anguish it causes *you*. Lay your anger at the foot of the cross. Let Him become "the grain, new wine and oil, enough to satisfy you fully." Nothing else can ever fill the void in your heart, except the Lord.

In his book, *Names of God*, Nathan Stone defined *Adonai* as *Lord*. He says that "lordship means complete *possession* on the one hand and complete *submission* on the other."[4] In addressing Jehovah as Adonai, you acknowledge God's complete possession of, and perfect right to, all that you are or have. Joseph knew God as Adonai. Paul knew God as Adonai. Now, God wants *you* to know Him as Adonai.

When you give Him your complete submission, accepting that you are His child and He knows what is best for your life, all of your expectations of Him will vanish.

Stress is a result of sin.

That is why Joseph was at peace with the Lord and his brothers. He trusted God for everything. Because Joseph had sought God's heart with confidence in the throne room, he could stand with peace and joy in the midst of terrible circumstances. He could praise God for sending him to Egypt as a slave so that years later his family would have food during a famine.

God is more concerned with your character than with your circumstances. In the flesh, we are just the opposite. We are more concerned with what is going on around us than with how our character is developing. But peace comes from within. God is glorified from our hearts.

Read Jeremiah 29:11-14 and ask the Lord to become real to you today as Adonai. Write out your prayer in the space below.

TRUTHS TO EMBRACE

_____

_____

_____

_____

_____

_____

Week Two, Day Five

STRESSED OUT!

That is why I am suffering as I am. Yet I am not ashamed, because I know whom I have believed, and am convinced that he is able to guard what I have entrusted to him for that day.

2 Timothy 1:12

Everybody is stressed. Even children talk about the stress in their lives. Stress is cited as one of the most common causes of many of the health problems our society faces. T-shirts, greeting cards, self-help sessions, seminars, books, and talk shows proclaim ways to relieve stress.

The bottom line is, stress is a result of sin. I don't know about you, but I find this distressing. It means that I'm trying to cover up my sin, but it still finds a way to manifest itself it through stress. Any sin, especially the ones we are trying to hide, can cause stress. Today, we will focus on two sins in particular: unforgiveness and broken relationships.

I kept saying I was trusting God (and I really thought I was), but in reality, I was stressed.

According to Luke 9:1-2, in what two ways did Jesus give the Twelve power and authority to heal the sick? _____
_____
_____

What caused the sickness referred to in James 5:14-16? _____
_____
_____

According to Mark 2:3-12, how did Jesus heal the paralytic? _____
_____
_____

God is always faithful to His Word.

Have you ever been so consumed with anger or unforgiveness in a broken relationship that the stress almost paralyzed you? What was the situation? Has it been resolved? How? _____
_____
_____
_____
_____

I am not suggesting that all illness is a result of sin. However, God's Word does say that some illness is caused from sin, and it can be manifested through symptoms of physical stress. Stress can manifest itself in many ways such as headaches, depression, anxiety, heart problems, stroke, muscle spasm, violent behavior, or excessive sleeping. Any of these behaviors can be paralyzing because they take our focus off of the Lord.

Some time ago, when I was asked to speak at a ladies retreat, I prayed for God to give me a word to speak that was totally from Him and nothing I contrived on my own. I prayed and waited, prayed and waited, and prayed and waited some more. Two days before I was to speak, I sat at my computer all day praying and waiting. I thought, *I'm ready, Lord. I've been patient, but we are running out of time.* The day came and went, and I still had no message. At the retreat the night before I was supposed to speak, I kept telling myself, *I'm just trusting the Lord to give me what to say.* But by the end of the praise and worship that night, the muscles in my neck were in such a spasm that I could not turn my head and the pain was terrible.

I kept saying I was trusting God (and I really thought I was), but in reality, I was stressed. The worst part was that with my neck problem, my stress was now an evident witness to all those near me of my lack of trust. I was looking at the circumstance instead of God's character. I was focused on the fact that time was running out, and I still did not have a word from the Lord. My focus needed to be Hebrews 13:5 where God tells us, *"Never will I leave you; never will I forsake you."*

Because God is always faithful to His Word, He gave me what I needed exactly when I needed it. As I was walking to the platform, I suddenly knew what to say. God doesn't always cut it that close. This particular time, He was teaching me about trust and how the lack of trust causes major health problems. The next time I was asked to speak, God gave me the material three months in advance (for which I praise His holy name!).

Write out Proverbs 13:12. _____
_____
_____
_____

Your Lord and Savior, Jesus Christ, understands how it feels to be wronged by someone you care about and who supposedly cares about you.

The Hebrew word translated *deferred* is *mashak,* meaning to be postponed.[5] The Greek word translated *heart* is *leb,* meaning the mind, the thinking, knowledge, reflection, memory, inclination, resolution, determination (of will), the seat of emotions, passions, and appetites, or the conscience.[6] The Greek word translated *sick* is *chalah,* meaning to make oneself sick or to be made weak.[7] The Greek word translated *longing* is *ta'avah,* meaning the longing of one's heart, a desire.[8]

Knowing that Jesus is our only hope, what happens when you postpone your hope in Jesus? _____

_____

_____

_____

_____

Besides being stressed out, what do you think it means to be made weak in the spiritual realm? _____

_____

_____

_____

Look at yesterday's definition of Adonai. What difference will your attitude toward forgiveness take when the longing of your heart, your desire, is to glorify Jesus Christ instead of focusing on your circumstances? _____

_____

_____

_____

Jesus was crucified at the insistence of His own people, some of the same people who had cheered Him during His triumphant entry into Jerusalem only one week earlier.

What does Luke 23:34 tell us He said? _____

_____

According to 1 Samuel 15:22-23, what does God desire from you? _____

_____

_____

Your Lord and Savior, Jesus Christ, understands how it feels to be wronged by someone you care about and who supposedly cares about you. He knows what a sacrifice it is to forgive, but the Lord commands us to obey His Word. Just as He Himself did, Jesus wants you to sacrifice yourself and what is most dear to you – not impersonal burnt offerings. In your natural self, your flesh cannot forgive. It is only when you are walking in the Holy Spirit that you can forgive the wrongs unjustly done to you.

What does Proverbs 16:25 say to you? _____

_____

The world says that we have a right to withhold forgiveness, but in the end the stress caused from that unforgiveness leads to a feeling of spiritual and physical death.

Trusting your life, your feelings, your hopes, and your disappointments to your Adonai takes away your stress and replaces it with the peace of God that passes all understanding.

What does God command in Philippians 4:6? _____
_____
_____

The word translated *anxious* is the Greek word *merimna'te,* meaning to be wrung in two directions at once.[9] Isn't that exactly the way stress makes us feel?!

What is God's promise to us in Philippians 4:7? _____
_____
_____

The word translated *guard* is the Greek military term, *phroureo,* meaning to protect by a military guard; to prevent a hostile invasion by watching and guarding; or to preserve one for the attainment of something.[10]

According to 2 Corinthians 10:3-5, how do we wage war? _____
_____
_____

One of our most effective weapons in this spiritual war is the weapon of forgiveness.

The word translated *peace* is the Greek word *eirene,* meaning a state of national tranquility, exception from the rage and havoc of war, or rest.[11] We are in a spiritual war and when we fight with the weapon of forgiveness, God's peace is our rest, our protection from the rage and havoc of war.

According to Matthew 11:28-30, when we are weary and come to Jesus, what does He give us? _____
_____
_____

When we take His yoke upon us, we are accepting Him as Adonai. We acknowledge God's complete possession of and perfect right to all that we are and have. Through this intimate relationship, we truly begin to know God and His love for us.

Write out 2 Timothy 2:12. _____
_____
_____
_____

Because Paul knew God personally and intimately, he trusted in His character, not His activity – this is especially important since we don't always understand the way God works.

What does Isaiah 55:8 tell us about God's ways? _____
_____
_____

Trusting your life, your feelings, your hopes, and your disappointments to your Adonai takes away your stress and replaces it with the peace of God that passes all understanding.

My friend, Susie, says, "Trust God and love people." People will hurt and disappoint you because they are only human, but Father God never will. Only He is worthy of your trust because only He is holy, righteous, perfect, and true.

Spend some time in prayer and ask God to reveal to you what is keeping you from trusting Him completely. Ask Him to give you the desire and the ability to trust Him in every situation. Give Him whatever is causing stress in your life. Remember that forgiveness does not mean that you were wrong and the offender was right. It is simply obedience to God's command and will cause you to live in peace and rest in His love and protection.

TRUTHS TO EMBRACE

_____
_____
_____
_____
_____
_____

Week 3

I NEED
A GAME PLAN

Week three will focus on our self-control. We tend to make excuses or justify our actions, but God always goes straight to the heart. Trusting our heavenly Father with the outcome of a situation begins with an act of our will, but the end result is peace. As if we don't have enough to do to take care of ourselves, many of us take up an offense against our family and friends. But this week, we will learn to respond rather than to react as we live in the reality of God's grace.

DAY 1
In My Defense…

DAY 2
But What If…?

DAY 3
Hot Potato

DAY 4
R-n-R: Response, not Reaction

DAY 5
Reality Check

IN MY DEFENSE...

"Would you discredit my justice? Would you condemn me to justify yourself?"

Job 40:8

We live in a society that justifies everything.

Every mother has a few pet peeves that she drills into her children. All four of my children would agree that I have stressed two of these pet peeves in particular. One: Use things in the manner in which they were intended – this way you will not break them or get hurt. Two: Do not base your behavior on the behavior of your brother or your friends – your behavior should be based on the Word of God and nothing else.

We live in a society that justifies everything. By shifting blame, we become a nation of victims. Trial lawyers argue that a crime is not the defendant's fault but is a result of his environment or bad parenting. We point our fingers at others in an attempt to justify our own behavior.

The problem is that we have forgotten our standard. Our standard should not be the laws of our nation, family values, school rules, or office criteria. Our standard is the Word of God. Our goal of righteousness is to be like the Lord Jesus Christ, not our next-door neighbor or Sunday school teacher.

When we try to justify our actions, we are trying to prove that we were right in our actions or words regardless of the consequence.

Why does Romans 3:19-24 say our righteousness can only come from Jesus? ____
_____
_____
_____
_____

Webster's dictionary defines *justify* as, "to show to be just, right, or in accordance with reason; to free from blame, declare guiltless; to supply good or lawful grounds for."[1] *Vine's Expository Dictionary* defines it as the "act of pronouncing righteousness, justification, acquittal from guilt."[2] When we try to justify our actions, we are trying to prove that we were right in our actions or words regardless of the consequence. It is a matter of pride. We want to justify our behavior so that we don't have to admit that we were wrong. We want to be acquitted from our guilt at the expense of others. It is almost impossible to have a healthy relationship with this kind of person.

Read Luke 18:9-14. What kind of person tries to justify his behavior? _____

_____

_____

_____

Is it possible to find a sufficient lawful reason for what we have done or said?

_____

In Matthew 12:37, what does God say about our words? _____

_____

_____

According to Job 15:6, what happens to our words when we try to justify ourselves?

_____

_____

According to Job 40:8, what do we do to God when we try to justify ourselves?

_____

_____

Look up the following verses to determine the only true place from which our justification comes and also how it comes.

Romans 5:15-18 _____

Romans 4:25 _____

Read Genesis 3:8-13.

After disobeying God's command, what was Adam and Eve's first reaction when God approached them? _____

_____

_____

When God confronted them with their actions, did they admit their guilt or try to justify their actions? _____

_____

_____

_____

Read the remainder of Genesis 3. Did God accept their justification for their actions and remove the consequences? _____

_____

According to Luke 16:15, we can justify ourselves to men, but what about God?

_____

_____

Read Luke 10: 25-37. What is the opposite of justification? _____

_____

When you try to justify your actions, your focus is yourself. When you have mercy on someone, your focus is on God, and then that person.

When you try to justify your actions, your focus is *yourself*. When you have mercy on someone, your focus is on God, and then that person. When Jesus died to justify you, His focus was on God. When God has mercy on you, the focus is solely on the Lord. *Vine's Expository Dictionary* defines *mercy* as "something that assumes need on the part of him who receives it, and resources adequate to meet the need on the part of him who shows it."[3]

When we accept Jesus as Lord and Savior, He justifies us to the Father. His grace covers all of our past, present, and future sin, because we could never adhere to the law and be good enough to deserve eternal life. Through His great mercy, He meets our need. Therefore, there is no need to justify ourselves. In fact, trying to justify ourselves is actually a slap in the face of God. It says that what Jesus did was not enough. It says that we think that in and of ourselves, we are good, righteous, and just. It is pride.

Accepting grace is facing our own depravity, knowing that apart from the grace of God, we truly are capable of anything.

Accepting grace is facing our own depravity, knowing that apart from the grace of God, we truly are capable of anything. Once we face our depravity and give God our pride, we can look anyone in the eye and say, meaning it with our heart, "I am sorry. I was wrong," because there is no more pretense of who we are apart from the grace of God. Also, by the very definition of the word *mercy*, we know that God will give us the resources to meet that need.

Fill in the following blanks.

Matthew 5:37 says, *Simply let your* _____ *be* _____, *and your* _____, _____; *anything beyond this comes from the evil one.*

By the same token, when we apologize, we should simply say, "I am sorry. I was wrong." Because, when we say, "I am sorry, but …" or, "I was wrong, but …," it is justification and that is sin. Adding the word "but" is a disclaimer. It says that we think it was really not our fault. It completely negates the apology.

What a difference when we accept that we were wrong and admit it to the person we wronged! This brings complete healing because there are no more excuses.

When we understand who we are in Christ Jesus, we no longer need to make excuses. We know that we are sinners saved by grace. Even though we are depraved, we are unconditionally loved and accepted by our heavenly Daddy, and nothing we ever say or do can change that fact.

Read Galatians 6:12-16. According to verse 16, when we become a new creation, what two things follow? _____

_____

_____

The act of God's saving us is mercy, and we experience peace as a result.

The act of God's saving us is mercy, and we experience peace as a result. This same principle is true when we have mercy on others. When we apologize without excuses to someone, we extend mercy to them by meeting their need; the result is peace.

Fill in the blanks with some of the justifications we use. The first one has been done for you.

- I'm sorry, but *I was just having a bad day.*
- I'm sorry, but _____

_____.

- I didn't mean to hurt you; it's just that _____

_____.

- I shouldn't have said that; it's just that sometimes you _____

_____.

Can you think of a time when someone apologized to you this way? How did it make you feel? _____

_____

_____

_____

Read Proverbs 25:11. What were the "apples of gold in settings of silver" that you longed to hear? Do you think that this would have brought peace to that relationship? _____

_____

_____

Sometimes we are placed in situations in which we feel the need to defend ourselves even though we have done nothing wrong.

In Mark 15:2-5, how did Jesus respond to Pilate? _____

_____

_____

Why do you think He did not defend Himself? _____

_____

Do you think this glorified God? Why or why not? _____

_____

_____

In the story of Job, God allowed Satan to come against Job, his family, and his possessions. Job lost his children, his material goods, and his health, yet he had done nothing to deserve it. Finally, Job sank to the low point of questioning God.

In Job 38:1-7, what did God say to Job? _____

_____

Read Job 42:1-6. How did Job respond to God? What brought about his change of heart? _____

_____

_____

_____

How different the situation becomes when we look through God's eyes! The difference comes from a commitment to the Lord, our Adonai, as we trust our life and circumstances to Him for His purpose and glory. Again, our focus must remain on God and not ourselves.

Read Job 42:10-16. What did God provide for Job in the end? _____

_____

_____

In Numbers 32, the Reubenites and Gadites settled for less than God's best by not trusting Him. Job trusted God, and his faith allowed him to settle in the "promised land."

Read Daniel 3.

What crime had Shadrach, Meshach, and Abednego committed? _____

_____

_____

Fill in the blank from verse 16: *Shadrach, Meshach, and Abednego replied to the king, "O Nebuchadnezzar, _____ before you in this matter."*

Why were they able to say this? _____

_____

Was God glorified through their witness? Why or why not? _____

_____

These young men had faith in God and in His divine purpose. He was their Adonai, and they trusted Him with their lives and circumstances. They knew God was able to save them. However, they did not know if it was His *will* to save them. Either way, they were at peace because they knew who they were: His dearly loved children. They also knew that when we let God be in control of our life, He is with us and unbinds us in the fires of life (verse 25). And like it says in verse 27, we will come out of the fire without the smell of fire on us. He is trustworthy.

Write out Exodus 14:13-14. _____

_____

_____

_____

What does this verse mean to you? Apply it to a fire through which you are currently going. _____

_____

_____

_____

Like Job, Shadrach, Meshach, and Abednego, will you commit to trusting God and allowing Him to be your defender in the fires of life? Give Him all your excuses and join in praise, saying:

> *To him who is able to keep you from falling and to present you before his glorious presence without fault and with great joy – to the only God our Savior be glory, majesty, power and authority, through Jesus Christ our Lord, before all ages, now and forevermore! Amen.*
>
> *Jude 1:24-25*

These young men had faith in God and in His divine purpose. He was their Adonai, and they trusted Him with their lives and circumstances.

TRUTHS TO EMBRACE

_____

_____

_____

_____

_____

_____

BUT WHAT IF...?

"Abba, Father," he said, "everything is possible for you. Take this cup from me. Yet not what I will, but what you will."

Mark 14:36

The idea of trusting God with my life and the people in it was very hard for me to accept because I'm a "fixer" who likes a plan.

My husband loves to work in the church nursery. He is great with kids of all ages, and it is obvious how much he enjoys them.

Our own four children are high maintenance and border on hyperactive. When they were young, I dreaded the Sunday that it was our turn to work in the nursery because I was exhausted. All week I would worry – *What if?* What if they got rowdy? What if we had too many kids to handle? What if we ran out of activities? What if the sermon went really long? The list went on. Nothing was ever as bad as I imagined. Yet I would work myself into such a state that after church I would go home and fall into bed from emotional exhaustion. My worry caused anxiety for me and havoc for my family.

Sound crazy? Well, often we do the same thing to the Father when we start thinking, *But what if...?*, instead of trusting Him with the outcome of our situation.

The idea of trusting God with my life and the people in it was very hard for me to accept because I'm a "fixer" who likes a plan. I don't mind change, but I want detailed directions about that change. I guess the bottom line is that I have a problem with *control!*

Read Proverbs 16:9. Write an example of a time you had a specific plan for your life but God determined your steps elsewhere. _____

_____

_____

Read Proverbs 16:25. Have you ever thanked God for not answering your prayer the way you fervently asked Him to? Why? _____

_____

_____

After God delivered the children of Israel from the bondage of slavery in Egypt, their disobedience caused them to spend forty years wandering in the wilderness before they crossed the Jordan River to live in the Promised Land. In his book, *Overcoming*

The more we know God, the easier it is to trust Him.

the Grasshopper Complex, Erwin Lutzer writes, "If Egypt represents the world, and the long excursion in the desert represents the discipline every one of us experiences, then the Jordan River represents the full surrender that must precede the lifelong task of knowing God."[4]

The more we know God, the easier it is to trust Him. To know Him as *Abba*, our heavenly Daddy, is one of the most intimate relationships we will ever experience. In Aramaic, the word *Abba* is an intimate term denoting a complete lack of fear and anxiety. It denotes someone in whom there is total and unreasoned trust. Slaves were forbidden to use this term; it was reserved only for family.

According to Romans 8:15, as *Abba's* child, what did we not receive? _____
_____
_____

What is the opposite of fear? _____

When God calls us to do something, fear makes us think, *But what if…?*

What does Mark 14:36 tell us Jesus said? _____
_____

Why do you think He was able to say this? _____
_____
_____

According to Deuteronomy 28:1-2, does God honor obedience? _____
_____

Sometimes, out of obedience, we must surrender ourselves — our circumstances, our friends, and our family – until we can truly trust from our heart and know that God will honor our obedience because His Word says He will. When we do this, we begin that lifelong task of intimately knowing our *Abba*.

Another word for surrender is *consecrate*.

Study the following scriptures to develop a definition for *consecrate*: Joshua 3:5; Ephesians 4:25-32; Hebrews 2:8; 1 Chronicles 29:3-5; Exodus 30:29; and Matthew 26:39. _____
_____
_____
_____

To consecrate means to dedicate to God. Consecration is totally selling out yourself to God and giving over your will to His. You are able to do this by faith because you know Him intimately and trust in His sovereignty. You consecrate your life and then God's use of your life sanctifies it. To sanctify your life means to set it apart from other uses to a particular use of God. Your life had another use, but now it belongs to God.

Consecration is totally selling out yourself to God and giving over your will to His.

An example would be when my discernment becomes consecrated to God. Instead of a critical spirit, it becomes the gift of discernment, sanctified to be used in ministry to glorify God. We consecrate our children, our marriage, our church, our hurtful situations, and the solutions to God by saying, *whatever it takes*. This cuts off the way we want things done (which for me is always the least costly, least embarrassing, quickest, and least painful solution). It means we have to come to the point where we say, *God, just work it out the way You see fit. We don't care about the cost.* It means saying, *Whatever, Lord. Whatever it takes.* To do this, we must first bind the religious spirit that tells us God wants us to be miserable, because that's a lie!

Read John 3:16 and describe God's love. _____
_____
_____

God loves His children with an agape love. Agape love actively seeks the highest good of another.

God can change our circumstances, but He is more concerned with changing our character.

Early in our marriage my husband and I did not share an active relationship with the Lord. For a while, I took the children to church and sat in my weekly ladies class. When he did start going to church with us, I longed for him to be the spiritual head of our household. A friend and I committed to pray together every morning at 9 AM for our husbands. We would call each other on the phone, kneel beside our husbands' bedsides, and pray.

I will never forget the day that she prayed with total abandon for God to raise up her husband as their spiritual head, no matter what it took. I gasped and wanted to interrupt her prayer by saying, "Are you crazy? God might do something awful to him, and you'll have to suffer the consequences." Fortunately, I kept my mouth shut and pondered what she said.

I could hear the abandoned trust in her voice. She intimately knew her *Abba* and trusted Him with her life and her husband. She knew that His ways were higher than her ways, so she did not need to worry. That day changed my life. It took some time, but eventually I was also able to consecrate my husband to the Lord by saying,

Whatever it takes, Lord. It was then that I began to see the Lord move in major ways in my husband's life. But like the case of Shadrach, Meshach, and Abednego, it no longer mattered what God *did*, because I trusted in who God *was*. God can change our circumstances, but He is more concerned with changing our character.

As difficult as it is to consecrate your husband or children, it is more difficult to consecrate yourself. To do so means laying your pride at the foot of the cross and allowing God to strip you of all ambition, agendas, and fear. You are no longer concerned about what others think of you or even what you think of yourself. Consecration is your saying, *Not my will, but Yours because You are my Lord and Savior.* It is your knowing that when you consecrate a hurtful situation to God, the outcome may be to suffer or to swallow your pride in order to glorify Him. It is your having such a trust in your *Abba* that whether He chooses to defend you or leave you in the fire, you will stay at peace, focused on Him no matter what – because you know He is there with you. It is your desire for Him to be glorified by the circumstances of your life no matter the personal cost to you. It is your returning your *Abba's* love with an agape love that actively seeks His highest good.

Read 1 Peter 2:19-25. What do you need to consecrate to the Lord? What is keeping you from giving Him control in this area? Consecrate it today and let the Lord govern your heart with the power of His divine grace. Only then will you experience healing from the hurt and freedom from the bondage that it brings.

TRUTHS TO EMBRACE

_____
_____
_____
_____
_____
_____

HOT POTATO

Do not take revenge, my friends, but leave room for God's wrath, for it is written: "It is mine to avenge; I will repay," says the Lord.

Romans 12:19

When you are hurt or upset, to whom do you run? Your spouse? A parent? Your friends? The next time you need someone in whom to confide, remember, the Lord is always the best person for the job. He is a haven of safety – One with whom you can share exactly how you feel and the depth of your pain. He can keep a secret, and He always knows what to do.

If you are married or a parent, you have a perfect example of why you should go to the Lord and no one else. Your parents don't need to know everything your spouse says or does wrong. Why? Because long after you two have reconciled, Mom and Dad will still be carrying that offense. If you are a parent, you know that it is much easier to forgive an offense against yourself than it is to forgive an offense against your children, because your protective mode kicks in. That's the very reason you also need to be careful about picking up someone else's offense – it is not your battle to fight.

As a Christian, every battle you fight is a spiritual battle also fought in the heavenlies for the glory and honor of the Lord Jesus Christ. Nothing you say or do is autonomous. It is all a reflection of the Holy Spirit that lives within you, of whether you are abandoned to serve God or yourself and your purpose.

The next time you need someone in whom to confide, remember, the Lord is always the best person for the job.

What meaning do the following verses have for you?

1 Samuel 17:47: _____

_____

2 Chronicles 20:15: _____

_____

What does Romans 12:19-21 tell us we are to do? _____

_____

_____

What is God's stand on revenge? _____

When we take on God's battle and seek revenge ourselves, what does it demonstrate about what we think of God? _____

_____

_____

Picking up someone else's offense is like accepting a hot potato. You need to pass it on quickly, or you'll get burned.

Picking up someone else's offense is like accepting a hot potato. You need to pass it on quickly, or you'll get burned. And the only person to whom the "hot potato" can be safely passed is Father God, because passing it to anyone else will only create more division and drag more people into the fire with you. It may seem noble to take up for someone and fight their battle, but when you do this, your focus is on yourself and what you can do on their behalf instead of on allowing God to work for His glory. It may feel good to be their champion, but the truth is, unless God has called you into that particular battle, you're in the wrong place at the wrong time.

What do the following scriptures say about God's ability and desire to fight for His people?

Deuteronomy 1:30 _____

_____

Deuteronomy 3:22 _____

_____

Deuteronomy 20:4 _____

_____

Nehemiah 4:20 _____

_____

Exodus 14:14 _____

_____

What are we to do? _____

_____

What can you do best when you are still? _____

_____

What battles are we to fight when called? _____

_____

The key here is to fight when God calls us, and not when our emotions get the best of us.

One Wednesday night at my church's prayer meeting, a long list of prayer requests was announced. As I looked around, I felt discouraged because the list was extensive, yet very few people bothered to write down these requests. I wondered if we were just going through the motions. Then, I remembered times when someone's prayer request had pierced my heart, and I didn't need to write it down because God wrote it on my heart. I realized then that God does not intend for us to fight every battle. We are to pick up only the offense that He hands us, and most important, we are to fight this battle in the spiritual realm, on our knees in prayer.

According to 2 Corinthians 10:4, with what kind of weapons do we fight? _____

_____

_____

According to 2 Samuel 22:35-40 and Psalm 144:1, what does God provide, besides weapons, before He sends us into battle? _____

_____

_____

You can stand assuredly on the battlefield of your Lord because the strength of a group depends on its leader.

The key here is to fight when God calls us, and not when our emotions get the best of us.

What does Psalm 24:8 say about the Lord? _____

_____

Who is the commander of the heavenly host? _____

What does James 4:1-12 say to you? _____

_____

How many churches have been divided because of fights and quarrels within? The important part is how the conflict is handled. Instead of corporately taking the problem to the Lord in prayer, members take sides by picking up offenses and talking among themselves to gain support. We seldom bring the whole issue into the open for corporate prayer.

Write out Proverbs 17:9. _____

_____

_____

Prayer is what covers an offense and promotes love. What is causing division in your life or in your church body? Make a commitment to take it to the Lord in prayer. Ask Him to give you a burden about whom or what to pray, including your church and your church leadership.

Division is the goal of the enemy. This is the Lord's battle. Ask Him to train your hands and teach you to pray before you champion any cause. Spend some time at His feet. If you are carrying someone else's offense, now is the time to place it on the altar of the Lord. Remember that the battle is the Lord's!

TRUTHS TO EMBRACE

_____
_____
_____
_____
_____
_____

R-n-R:
RESPONSE, NOT REACTION

The tongue has the power of life and death, and those who love it will eat its fruit.

Proverbs 18:21

I have wondered for years if God called me to the "ministry of screw ups." It seems that most of my life has been spent doing or saying the wrong thing and then trying to correct it. I know that through much of this God was glorified. His hand was obviously on my life as I was convicted to do His will. However, it is still embarrassing when I am not a consistent witness for the Lord. As Christians, we are always witnessing: We can either witness as a life abandoned to God – which glorifies Him – or we can witness as a life lived to self. A person whose life is lived in the flesh reacts to everything and everyone including God.

Lately, my prayer has been that I will respond – not react. Our goal should be to respond to God, to situations, and to people correctly the first time. We should be witnesses that glorify Him the first time He asks. Does this sound too hard? Are you thinking that it might be possible – after you have walked with the Lord a long time and become really mature? The good news is that we are under grace. You do not have to work at being a "better" Christian. It is just a matter of giving God control of your life and asking Him to change you because you cannot do it alone.

Read Luke 1:26-38.

Did Mary react or respond? _____
_____

How long did it take her? _____

Knowing that she was a young girl, how would you describe her relationship with the Lord? _____
_____
_____

Knowing that everything you do for Christ is done through grace, what can you apply from this passage to your life and walk with the Lord? _____
_____
_____

As Christians, we are always witnessing: We can either witness as a life abandoned to God – which glorifies Him – or we can witness as a life lived to self.

You do not have to work at being a "better" Christian. It is just a matter of giving God control of your life and asking Him to change you because you cannot do it alone.

Read Luke 1:46-55. How was God glorified? _____
_____

God looks for availability,

not perfection, in the lives

of His children.

God looks for availability, not perfection, in the lives of His children. In fact, He uses the foolish things of the world to confound the wise (1 Cor. 1:27). In other words, God's power is even more evident when He works through someone who does not have natural talent, because then it is obvious that the work is done completely by God and not at all by that person. We just need to be available and abandoned to God's purposes so that we respond and don't react. However, all of us reactors are in good company, and there is hope for improvement. It's a humbling thought!

Read John 18:1-11.

Did Peter react or respond to the circumstances in which he found himself? ____
_____
_____

How long did it take him? _____

Knowing that Peter was not just a disciple, but one of the inner circle, how would you describe his relationship with the Lord? _____
_____

How was God glorified?_____
_____

Let's take a closer look at John 18:10-11. Write it in the space provided.
_____
_____
_____
_____

Read Matthew 26:50-54. Does God need our help? Why? _____
_____

In Matthew 26:51 and John 18:10, the word translated *sword* is the Greek word, *machaira*, meaning a short sword or dagger knife used for hand-to-hand combat.[5]

This is the same word used in Ephesians 6:17: *The sword of the* _____, *which is the* _____ *of* _____.

When we use the sword of the Spirit, to whom does this sword really belong?

_____

_____

In John 18:11, whose sword did Jesus tell Peter to put up? _____

_____

_____

According to John 18:11 and Matthew 26:53-54, whose battle was this to fight?

_____

_____

According to what we learned yesterday, what happens when we pick up someone else's offense and battle it ourselves in our own strength? _____

_____

_____

What did Jesus tell Peter to do with his sword? _____

The Greek word translated *put* is *ballo,* meaning to throw or let go of a thing without caring where it falls, or to give over to one's care, uncertain about the result.[6] We are not called to fight in our own strength with our own weapons. In fact, Jesus commands us to throw away our weapons even though we are uncertain about the result. We must trust Him with all that we have — knowing that He will provide for all that we need.

What do Romans 8:15 and Galatians 4:6 call us? _____

As Christians, we are very good at quoting scripture out of context for our own purposes or to point out the sins of others. A problem arises when we do this with our own sword, in our own strength. God does not need our help. He is perfectly able to convict His children of sin without our assistance or advice. We must learn to fight only the battles He chooses for us, using His weapons and not our own. This means we must learn to respond — not react.

The best and safest place for Christians to be is on their knees in prayer for the people and situations that are of concern. When we try to correct fellow Christians in our own strength, our reaction usually causes them to feel condemned. But when God uses us to correct another Christian in His strength, our response causes conviction because it is in His timing and under His anointing.

Read Proverbs 18:21.

The best and safest place for Christians to be is on their knees in prayer for the people and situations that are of concern.

When you wield the sword of the Spirit, the Word of God, what does your tongue bring forth? _____

_____

When you wield your own sword, your own words, what does your tongue bring forth? _____

What do you think the fruit would be? _____

Write Proverbs 18:21, substituting the word *division* for *death* and *reconciliation* for *life*. _____

_____

When Peter cut off the ear of the high priest's servant, he was cutting off the servant's ability to hear the Word of God. We do much the same thing today. When we wield our own swords, we turn both Christians and non-Christians away from the Word of God and the church. Do we have good intentions? Yes. Does that make it okay? Absolutely not!

As a young (and immature!) Christian, I was involved in a church as the nursery coordinator. My pastor was not good with small children and did not place a priority on their nurturing, but as the nursery coordinator, it was *my* priority! He and I had several disagreements about ministry to the children under my care.

One evening, I went to a meeting with him and several church leaders. I found every scripture in the Bible on children and Jesus' attitude toward them. At the meeting, I wielded my "sword" in front of the church leaders. I was going to show, "in the name of Jesus," just how wrong he was. My intentions were right. Unfortunately, I had chosen to fight on the wrong field – I should have fought the battle on my knees. It took twelve years for us to reconcile. God had to deal with both of our hearts, and when the time was right, the sword of the Spirit brought conviction and reconciliation to our relationship.

Because of the immediate timing and emotion involved, it is probably hardest to resist reacting when we find ourselves under attack and unjustly accused of something. But this is an opportunity to either react or respond.

In Acts 2:5-13, of what were Peter and the other disciples unjustly accused?

_____

_____

_____

In Acts 2:14-41, did Peter react or respond? _____

_____

Do you think the people felt conviction or condemnation? Why? _____

_____

_____

_____

How was God glorified? _____

How did Peter's actions and words effect different outcomes in Acts 2:14-41 and
John 18:10-11? _____

_____

_____

*All will not be happy,
fun, and easy in your
life simply because you
are filled with the Holy
Spirit and responding in
a godly way.*

All will not be happy, fun, and easy in your life simply because you are filled with
the Holy Spirit and responding in a godly way. Even though you are yielded to your
heavenly Father and His time and purpose, you may never know the reason for the
outcome or how God is using you; however, you will know His peace and strength
throughout the circumstance.

Read Acts 6:8-7:60.

Do you believe Stephen was walking in God's will? Why? _____

_____

Did Stephen respond or react to the charges? Explain your answer._____

_____

Do you think the people felt conviction or condemnation? Why?_____

_____

_____

How was God glorified? _____

_____

Through God's grace, how can you apply this passage to your life and walk with the
Lord? _____

_____

_____

_____

Write Proverbs 18:13 in your own words. _____

_____

_____

_____

Now is the time for a little R-n-R. Has there been a situation in your life in which you reacted instead of responded? Ask the Lord what you need to do in order for reconciliation to take place, then take a deep breath, lay down your pride, and do it. Healing is worth whatever pain or discomfort it takes to reconcile.

```
┌─────────────────────────────────────────────────┐
│                                                   │
│           T R U T H S   T O   E M B R A C E       │
│                                                   │
│   _____   │
│   _____   │
│   _____   │
│   _____   │
│   _____   │
│   _____   │
│                                                   │
└─────────────────────────────────────────────────┘
```

Week Three, Day Five

REALITY CHECK

Immediately, something like scales fell from Saul's eyes, and he could see again.

Acts 9:18

A few years ago God healed me of insecurity. I had spent most of my life feeling as though I didn't fit in or measure up to the standards of those around me. I often sat in familiar groups feeling totally isolated because I had put up protective walls around myself. I had backed away, even though in reality I had never moved. As time went on and I focused on my insecurity, I grew more and more miserable. I prayed for God's healing, and for a while I felt a little better. But by no means was I well.

One day at a Bible study, my heavenly Father sent two prayer warriors to pray for me. My life irrevocably changed that day. As they prayed, I gave the Lord my insecurity, and He replaced it with His love. When I opened my eyes, everything looked different. The light was brighter, the grass was greener, and the sky was bluer. Why? Because I had been looking through the stronghold of insecurity, and now I was looking through my strong tower, Jesus Christ.

A stronghold can be a way of thinking through which everything is filtered and comes out distorted and bent.

As we learned earlier in this study, a stronghold can be a way of thinking through which everything is filtered and comes out distorted and bent. It is like looking through glasses with red lenses. Even though the sky is blue, it appears red. Only when you take off the tinted lenses and look clearly at the sky will you see its true color.

The same is true of our strongholds. They become our dominant focus, even as Christians. Every word and action we see or hear is filtered through our stronghold and comes out distorted and bent. Only when we give our stronghold completely to Jesus and let Him heal us, will we see and hear clearly.

What does Proverbs 18:10 say the name of the Lord is? _____

_____

When we run to Him and are covered by Him, what happens to us?

_____

_____

In my mid-forties, my eyes have started to weaken. At night, I sometimes have difficulty seeing to drive. I can see okay — I just can't read the street signs until I am passing them, and sometimes I can't see our driveway! When I renewed my driver's license, I passed the eye exam just as I am. So by worldly standards, I can see just fine and, therefore, do not need glasses. But how do I explain this to my husband when I miss the driveway and turn into a ditch? How do I explain to my family that while they were sleeping in the car, I drove 100 miles out of our way because I couldn't read the road signs?

The bottom line is that my eyes do not focus properly and everything I see is distorted. On the surface I look fine and I can manage to get around, but in reality my driving could be dangerous to me and to those around me. It sounds just like a stronghold of sin, doesn't it?

Before our last family vacation, I got glasses. The first night I wore them, I thought, *Hey, who turned the lights on out here? Were the letters on the signs always that big and clear?* Through my new lenses, I was able to see clearly and was no longer a danger to others or myself. It was like seeing life and truth through my strong tower, Christ Jesus.

Read Acts 8:1-3 and Acts 9:1-2. Was Saul seeing the truth? Why? _____

_____

_____

_____

It is important to understand that when someone is looking through a stronghold, that stronghold affects their reality. Often this reality is involuntarily created as a protection against the hurts or sin they carry. As a persecutor of the early church, Saul believed that he was protecting his beliefs. Nothing could convince him otherwise. Acts 8 recounts how Paul (Saul) listened to Stephen as Stephen spoke the truth to the Sanhedrin, yet he stood by giving his approval as he watched Stephen being stoned to death.

Read Acts 9:3-22. What did it take to change Saul? Who was the only One who could touch Paul's heart and change him? _____

_____

_____

_____

Who was the instrument the Lord used to minister healing to Saul? _____

_____

Did Ananias go to Saul on his own agenda to fix this sinner? _____

_____

How did you feel when you read verse 15? _____

_____

_____

Without the grace of God, we are capable of committing any sin and descending to the depths of depravity.

I don't know about you, but I felt convicted. How many times have I known God wanted me to do something, yet I wanted to discuss it with Him first. God didn't want to discuss this with Ananias. He simply said, "Go!" The Greek word used here, *poreuomai*, marks the end of a court case or the end of a conversation.[7] Ananais had given his life to Jesus, but when the call came to go to Saul, he hesitated. The Father God was very firm with Ananias, because he was reacting to what he already knew about Saul and not responding to his Father.

When Ananias was obedient and fought the battle that God chose for him, what was the outcome in Saul's life? _____

_____

_____

When the scales literally fell from Saul's eyes, the scales dropped off his spiritual eyes as well. As a result, Saul was never the same again. Saul came to know his Savior and Lord in an intimacy that few have equaled. In retrospect, would Saul have had the same impact if he had not walked that same road? Probably not. We may not understand God's plan, but we can always trust it.

It is hard enough to deal with our own strongholds and depravity, but we must also deal with those of other people as well. To respond to others under the reign of the Spirit, we must first be acutely aware that without the grace of God, we are capable of committing any sin and descending to the depths of depravity. Next, we must pray that God will fill us with grace and love so that we will not react in the flesh.

My mother and I have never been close. For most of my life, I have anguished over how I could make her understand my intentions. It seemed she always mis-understood my words or motives. I have fretted and worried for years about how I could have said something better. I have spent hours thinking that if I could just explain again or if I could just do this or that differently, then maybe she would understand.

One desperate day, I counseled with a godly lady at my church. I wanted to make sense of this relationship and get advice grounded in the Word of God. She listened to me talk about my past and our relationship. Then she said, "Your mother creates her own reality. Nothing you say or do can change what she thinks because she hears everything through a stronghold." What a revelation!

I felt as though a huge weight had been lifted off me. For the first time in my life, I realized that it wasn't all me. I could never be good enough, thoughtful enough, or eloquent enough to satisfy my mother, because everything I did or said was filtered through her stronghold and therefore came out distorted and twisted.

Read Acts 13:49-52. What can you glean from this passage? _____

_____

_____

_____

Dealing with someone who creates his or her own reality can be very frustrating and hurtful. However, when someone misunderstands you or your intentions because of their stronghold, your must put your focus on God and not on the other person's perception of reality.

Where do you go from there? It all depends on God's direction for you and your situation. God separated my mother and me for a time.

Sometimes God separates us for a time so that we can heal and regain our strength. Sometimes He may also need to get us alone to teach us individually.

Read Genesis 13:5-9. Why did Abram separate from his nephew Lot? _____

_____

_____

According to Genesis 13:14, when did the Lord speak to Abram? _____

_____

_____

Sometimes God has to separate us from family or friends in order to get us to listen to Him and be teachable.

Read Genesis 27:41-45. From whom did Jacob flee? Why? _____

_____

_____

Read Genesis 35:1-7. During the time Jacob was separated from his brother, what did God do?

_____

_____

Sometimes God separates us for a time so that we can heal and regain our strength.

Sometimes God separates us from our family or friends in order to accomplish His higher purpose.

Sometimes God has to separate us in order to protect us from an abusive family member.

Read Genesis 45:4-11. Why and how was Joseph separated from his family? ____
_____

_____

Sometimes God separates us from our family or friends in order to accomplish His higher purpose. Knowing that God may separate us to protect us, heal us, teach us, or use us for His greatest glory enables us to respond in a godly manner to those who have hurt us.

Remember, God is interested in the attitude of your heart — not merely your outward behavior. He may never bring that person back into your life, but He wants you to be willing to extend His grace and have compassion regardless.

Remember, God is interested in the attitude of your heart — not merely your outward behavior.

Read 2 Corinthians 6:3-13. In verse 12 the word translated *affection* is the Greek word *splanchna*, which means with tender mercies and inward affections.[8] Using this information, write this verse in your own words. _____
_____

_____

Read 2 Corinthians 12:9-10. According to these verses, how is this accomplished?
_____

_____

In 2 Corinthians 10:3-5, how does the Word of God say that strongholds are demolished?
_____

_____

_____

No matter what the circumstance, God always desires for us to respond with grace. This is not natural or easy, but it is possible. To do this, we need to see clearly. Our personal reality check should be to ask the Lord to remove the blinders from our eyes so that we focus only on Jesus Christ. When He is our focus, we begin to see everything in a different light. Those that persecute us will be perceived through His eyes of grace, and we will begin to experience joy in the midst of difficult circumstances.

I am in one of the busiest times of my life. When I was younger, I was able to focus on many things at once, but not so now! I must be getting older because I can no longer focus on everything that is going on in my life. However, I find that if I stay focused on God, everything else pales in importance. I experience much more joy by simply trusting Him with the circumstances – and besides, He handles them much better than I do anyway!

Some of you have broken relationships and difficult circumstances in your lives that have caused you great pain. I am not minimizing what you have been through, but I am praying that you will turn it over to the Lord so that He can begin to heal you.

Ask God to give you the desire to trust Him with your feelings and with the entire situation. Consecrate it to Him and ask Him to walk sovereignly through it. You can trust your *Abba* to always actively seek your highest good. He loves you very much. Write your prayer to Him below.

TRUTHS TO EMBRACE

_____

_____

_____

_____

_____

_____

Week 4

THE BARRIERS

In week four we will explore the barriers in our lives. We put barriers on our reconciliation with God through legalism, our control, and forms of godliness. Our effectiveness as God's ambassadors to a lost world has barriers through worldly business codes that we have integrated into the church, our pious attitudes, our lack of approachability, and the masks we wear with others. I pray that this week, we will learn to "get real" in the body of Christ.

DAY 1
Boxed in

DAY 2
Power Dressing

DAY 3
Bartender, Please Help Me

DAY 4
Break Down the Walls

DAY 5
Take Off the Mask

BOXED IN

It does not, therefore, depend on man's desire or effort, but on God's mercy.

Romans 9:16

True godliness is taking a risk, doing a new work with no expectations, letting God be in control, and focusing on Him.

A popular Christian saying today is, "Don't put God in a box." Yet this is something we do all the time, "in the name of Jesus," with our outer forms of godliness. These outer forms of godliness seem spiritual but lack true power. It is doing what has always been done or what others expect of us. It is being in control; it is focusing on the situation. Our outer forms of godliness depend on our desires, efforts, or talents. But true godliness is taking a risk, doing a new work with no expectations, letting God be in control, and focusing on Him.

What does the scripture tell us in Romans 9:16? _____

_____

_____

A WOMAN NAMED MARTHA; HER SISTER CALLED MARY

Let's examine the story of Mary and Martha to see the ways that well-meaning Christians "put God in a box" and how this creates division and therefore inhibits our ministering reconciliation.

Read Luke 10:38-42. Fill in the columns with the qualities of Mary and Martha

Forms and methods of godliness/Martha	True godliness/Mary

As you study scripture, you will learn that there is meaning in every word God uses. Nothing is written by accident or as filler. The word *Martha*, of Aramaic origin, means mistress or rebellious.[1] Did you notice that scripture says, *a woman* named *Martha* and *her sister* called *Mary*? The word *name* in the Greek language refers to the thought or feeling which is aroused in the mind by mentioning, hearing, or remembering that word.[2] Even though Martha had good intentions in serving the Lord, she was rebellious. She was a mistress to outward forms of godliness. She had her own agenda for herself and her sister. Verse 40 tells us that Martha was distracted by all the preparations. How many times do we become distracted by the preparations, by the serving, by the ministry, and get our focus off of the Lord?

Can you think of a time when you became distracted by preparations? _____
_____
_____
_____

We have become so polished in our church services and programs that God could leave our midst and programs would run for a long time without anyone even noticing. The problem is that without God there is no power – we are just a country club with interesting activities, and lives will not be changed. We need to let go of our control and allow God to take over. He must be our focus in the midst of the preparation and service. God does not call us to do everything. We are the body of Christ, and it takes every part of the body working together to be healthy and whole. Too often, a few people do everything at church, and then they either burn out or become too controlling.

Are you on several committees? If so, please prayerfully consider why. Are you there to see that things are done to your standards? If you are doing more than one job, it could mean that someone else in the body of Christ is not being allowed to serve.

Part of our responsibility is to invite all of the body to participate. Many times people just need to be asked. Remember that we should serve out of availability and not ability.

Write 1 Corinthians 1:26-31 in your own words. _____
_____
_____
_____
_____

Part of the reason we need to limit our involvement is that we can become so busy serving that we have no time to spend with the Father in personal worship, praise, and teaching. The Greek word translated *called* is *kaleo*. It means to call anyone, invite, or summon, used particularly of the divine call to partake of the blessing of redemption.[3] Beloved, we are invited to partake of the blessing of redemption. That

The problem is that without God there is no power – we are just a country club with interesting activities, and lives will not be changed.

God does not call us to do everything. We are the body of Christ, and it takes every part of the body working together to be healthy and whole.

If you are doing more than one job, it could mean that someone else in the body of Christ is not being allowed to serve.

Serving Him simply comes out of the overflow of our hearts.

blessing is that by being co-heirs with Christ Jesus, we have uninhibited access to our heavenly Father. He invites us, like Mary, to sit at His feet while He teaches us. He is our Teacher, our *Rabboni*. We have one-on-one communion with God almighty. He invites us to come boldly into his throne room with our hurts, our joys, our concerns, and our questions. There are *no barriers!* This is what we were called to do. Serving Him simply comes out of the overflow of our hearts.

When we get our focus off of God, one of the repercussions is stress.

How would you describe Mary and Martha's stress levels and why? _____
_____
_____
_____

Read John 12:1-8.

What are the emphases of this passage? _____
_____
_____

What role does each person play?

Martha _____
_____

Lazarus _____
_____

Mary _____
_____

Judas _____
_____

How does Jesus respond to Judas' concern? _____
_____

How does Jesus respond to Martha's request in Luke 10:40-42? _____
_____
_____

Have you ever gone to the Lord with a similar request? _____
_____

What was His answer? _____
_____

The Greek word for *let alone* is *aphiemi*. It means to set free, to give up a debt, to forgive, not to hinder, or to depart from one and leave him to himself so that all mutual claims are abandoned.[4] Martha and Judas were trying to hinder Mary from worshipping the Lord. They both inferred that she owed a debt of service that she was ignoring by spending time with Jesus.

They were both making a claim on her time and property. They both put God in a box by saying there was one correct way to serve God. On the surface this may have seemed like godliness, but in reality they are just forms of godliness.

Where was their focus? _____
_____

Where was Mary's focus? _____
_____

What are some forms of godliness we have in the church today? _____
_____

As an immature Christian, I was part of a mainline church that started a Sunday night service called "The Healing Service." I was upset because I did not like the implications. We had never had such a service in our church, and I didn't think that our manmade by-laws approved of this format. We had always done a standard, safe Sunday night service and I guess, in my heart, I was more concerned with the presentation than God's desire. My focus was wrong. The worst part was that I never even went on Sunday nights, but I thought that now I couldn't even go if I wanted to because of this weird service. I complained to a woman at church who went to the service and she looked at me and said, "What do you think we are doing? If it was weird, then I wouldn't be there." I finally got enough courage to go, and when I did, I found out I was so wrong. It was a service of loving Christians, focused on the Lord, who took the time to pray with each other. Ignorance is not always bliss.

I want to spend my life focused on the Lord Jesus Christ. I want to be open to the Holy Spirit with a prepared heart. I want to be more interested in God than in the movement of God. Most importantly, I want my thoughts, decisions, and actions to be based only on what the Word of God says and not on manmade rules or traditions. I want to live my life in God's grace and mercy.

I want to spend my life focused on the Lord Jesus Christ. I want my thoughts, decisions, and actions to be based only on what the Word of God says and not on manmade rules or traditions.

Write out Romans 9:16. _____
_____
_____

Summarize today's lesson and write your own response to the Lord's teaching as, like Mary, you spend time sitting at His feet.

TRUTHS TO EMBRACE

_____
_____
_____
_____
_____
_____

POWER DRESSING

Therefore, as God's chosen people, holy and dearly loved, clothe yourself with compassion, kindness, humility, gentleness and patience.

Colossians 3:12

Many people dress a certain way to command power or respect. In the business world the term "the suits" refers to men (or women) of power, education, and influence. They are the lawyers, CEOs, and other powerful people who lead, make decisions, and influence business agendas in major ways.

When you have an important meeting, normally you will wear your best and most professional clothes to make an impression that you are knowledgeable and "a force to contend with."

Amazingly, we act differently depending upon how we are dressed. Sometimes I run into the grocery store without makeup and in old clothes. But if I see someone I know, I just want to hide. Why? It makes me feel inferior and allows people to see my every blemish, scar, and imperfection, not the "image" I see of myself. But I have noticed that this is when people want to talk most!

It is when we are vulnerable, non-threatening, and open that we become approachable.

A dear friend of mine recently changed churches after moving to a new neighborhood. She visited with a woman at church who made an interesting comment that I cannot forget. The woman said that the reason she attended that church was because it was casual, and the pastor wore slacks and a shirt to preach on Sunday morning. She said that she felt as though she could talk to him if she had an issue. "The suits" intimidated her because they made her feel inferior. His clothing made him seem like a "regular" person.

Her comments reminded me of several women's conferences in which I have been involved. Our brochures told attendees that the event was casual, yet all of us in leadership dressed up. Why? It gave us confidence. We were *power dressing* as the world teaches us! With pious attitudes, we were attempting to present an image of authority, knowledge, and leadership. I wonder how many women left that day feeling inferior or that they didn't quite "make the mark." You see, what we had inadvertently said was that they needed to "clean up" a little nicer to be as spiritual as we were.

When you have an important meeting, normally you will wear your best and most professional clothes to make an impression that you are knowledgeable and "a force to contend with."

Read Galatians 6:11-16.

Paul, more than any of the other apostles, understood grace.

It is interesting that Paul makes an issue of the fact that he is writing the last part of this letter in his own hand. Most of his letters were dictated to a secretary. Paul, more than any of the other apostles, understood grace. He knew firsthand the emptiness and devastation in his own life and the lives of those he touched because of his zeal for the law apart from grace. I like to think that in his passion, he might have just grabbed the pen and paper from his scribe to share the grace of God with us.

To the lives we touch, what is the difference between compelling them to be circumcised or allowing God to draw them into His light? _____

_____

_____

_____

We cannot drive someone to salvation or conviction of sin. When we attempt to do this in our own strength, the only thing they will experience is condemnation. It doesn't matter how good our intentions are; the only thing that brings true repentance is being drawn by the Father.

Write out John 6:44-45. _____

_____

_____

_____

_____

Although God is perfectly capable of convicting sin without our help, He sometimes chooses to use us as His vessel.

We are drawn by the Father to Jesus for salvation; then He draws us to His teaching as He works His refining process in our lives. God, the Holy Spirit within us, teaches us. Through this teaching, we are brought under conviction, which leads to repentance. This draws us closer to Jesus Christ, and His likeness is produced in us. Although God is perfectly capable of convicting sin without our help, He sometimes chooses to use us as His vessel. However, we must be walking very close to Him to know the times He calls us to be His vessel and the times when He calls us to quietly be a prayer intercessor for a person or situation.

According to 1 John 5:16, when we see someone commit a sin, what is the first thing we are to do? _____

_____

Have you ever placed your standards or convictions on someone else just to save your own skin, to avoid "being persecuted for the cross of Christ?" Maybe you expected godly precepts of them, and when they did not meet your expectations, you were disappointed, hurt, or angry, which caused a division between you. By the world's standard you were justified in your behavior, but God calls us to extend His grace. Grace is defined as unmerited favor. Grace is getting what we do not deserve because Jesus took upon Himself what we deserve – death and separation from God.

Think about your past relationships and then fill in the following blanks.
By placing my expectations on _____, I was trying to compel, force, or drive them to be "circumcised."

What does Galatians 6:13 say about those who try to force others to be circumcised?

_____

_____

_____

The worst part of looking back at those situations is recognizing the times when that person submitted to circumcision, and we were so proud to have helped "change" them.

In Galatians 6:13-14, what does Paul say about "boasting?" _____

_____

_____

_____

_____

The word *boast* in the Greek is *kauchaomai,* meaning to glory with or without a reason on account of a thing or in a thing.[5]

What is the difference in focus between the *glory* of verses 13 and 14 of Galatians 6?

_____

_____

Read Philippians 3:1-9. Do you see any similarities between these verses and Galatians 6:11-16? If so, what? How critical do you think Paul considered this concept to be? _____

_____

_____

_____

_____

_____

Only the Father can "draw" us.

As I look back at the controversies and need for reconciliation in my life, I see one common cause – putting my standards, or even God's standards, on someone else and trying to "drive" them into meeting those standards. This very often created division and put the focus on me and not the Lord. Were my intentions good? Yes, most of the time. I understood God's precepts and wanted others to behave accordingly. What I missed was that I cannot force anyone to God or to godly behavior. Only the Father can "draw" us. He blesses us beyond measure by drawing us to Himself and refining us through His teaching. However, the refiner's process is certainly not finished, and we cannot even boast like Paul to having followed the letter of the law.

I was a misfit expecting everyone else to be fit, especially in the areas that I had begun to grasp. There were even times when God worked in the lives of those I touched despite me, and there were times when my pride gloried in what "I" had done.

Praise God for the times He let my words fall on deaf ears. These times were so confusing because I knew I was right, and yet I saw the situation continue to spiral downward. What I did not understand was God's perfect timing. In His sovereignty, God brings about the course of events to point us to Him and glorify His holy name. Then, when He draws us into conviction, He will be the only One to receive the glory.

What do John 9:1-3, John 11:4, Romans 8:18, and Ephesians 1:11-12 say about our lives, circumstances, and God's timing and sovereignty? _____
_____
_____
_____

According to John 9:1-3, John 11:4, Romans 8:18, and Ephesians 1:11-12, when someone wrongs us or does not respond to us in love and grace, how are we to look at the situation? _____
_____
_____
_____

We are called to trust in God and extend His love and grace.

Read 2 Corinthians 3:7-11. What is the difference between the glory of administering the law and the grace of Jesus Christ? _____
_____
_____

Read John 9:13-16. What happened to the Pharisees when they were more focused on the letter of the law than on God? _____

_____

_____

When we become legalistic about God's precepts, we create division. We're dressing in our own power rather than the power of the Lord. We revere rules over God almighty.

Instead of "power dressing" as the world teaches, how does Colossians 3:12 tell us to dress? _____

_____

_____

Let's look at the Greek definitions of the qualities in which we are to clothe ourselves:

Compassion - (*splagchnon*) tender mercies, a heart of compassion[6]

Kindness - (*oiktirmos*) kindness, integrity[7]

Humility - (*tapeinophrosune*) having a humble opinion of oneself, a deep sense of one's moral littleness[8]

Gentleness - (*prautes*) meekness, which is strength under control[9]

Patience - (*makrothumia*) patience, constancy, perseverance, slowness in avenging wrongs[10]

I know that this is a hard lesson, because it was the most difficult for me to write. I must walk down the road before I can write about it. Nothing in this lesson comes from a pious heart that knows the correct thing to do and has always done it. I share with you from a heart broken for the ways I have not loved my God in the past, and the precious brothers and sisters that crossed my path. There is hope for us; He is the Lord Jesus Christ. Praise God that we are all saved and sanctified by grace.

How has the Lord touched your heart today?

TRUTHS TO EMBRACE
_____
_____
_____
_____
_____
_____

BARTENDER, PLEASE HELP ME

Having loved his own who were in the world, he now showed them the full extent of his love.
John 13:1

In the summer of 1998, God gave me a vision based on John 13:1 for a day of pampering for the women of our church. For one day, we turned our educational space into a health spa with volunteers trained in giving manicures, massages, facials, makeovers, and foot massages.

The rooms were beautifully decorated with candles and serene music for a very restful time. Each woman could sign up for several treatments. We even had speakers on God's love and foot washing. It was an incredible day!

The purpose of this day was to teach our ladies a principle about God's love and service in a very tangible way. Because God's love cannot be earned or bought, the entire day was offered free of charge.

God works in mysterious ways. If we will just extend His love and grace, He will do the conviction.

My heart was broken by responses from some of the women who would not attend. Some said that they could not take a day for themselves because they just did not deserve it. Some said that they would come if they could pay for the treatments, but they could not accept it for free. Some didn't mind serving, but they couldn't allow someone else to serve them.

The reason it broke my heart was because this is exactly how many people feel about the Father's love. They think they need to earn it or get cleaned up first. Some feel more comfortable trying to fit in by working as a servant, but they don't know how to let someone serve them. These are lies of the enemy. Unfortunately, many well-meaning Christians not only believe this lie, but also perpetuate it.

When we put stipulations on how things need to be, we make ourselves, and others, feel they don't measure up and cannot be a part of the group. Unfortunately, their fears are well founded. Too many times in the church, when someone is honest about their struggles, we ostracize them instead of extending God's love and mercy.

But God works in mysterious ways. If we will just extend His love and grace, He will do the conviction. Too often, we convict in our own strength, and cause condemnation and division; but when God convicts, true change and repentance take place.

Our attitudes drive them to secular sources (like the local bartender) to whom they can tell their problems, because there they can talk without fear of judgment. It's time that the church takes a realistic view of its own depravity and realizes that truly except for the grace of God, it could be them on that barstool.

Not one of us is above any sin. We were all bought with the price of Jesus' death on the cross, because not one of us could be righteous enough to deserve eternal life. Only through God's great grace and mercy, did Jesus take our death sentence and give us right standing before the holy and righteous God almighty.

Read John 13:1-17.

In verse 1, the Greek word translated *extent* is *telos*. It means the end to which all things relate, the aim or the purpose.[11]

According to 1 John 4:16, what is God? _____
_____
_____

God is love. Without love, there is no manifestation of God in our lives. God loves others through us, and God loves us through others. We don't have to know how; we don't have to have training; we simply have to trust Him and allow Him to work through us. The amazing part is that our hearts will go into overdrive for the Lord and for those around us when we allow God's love to flow through us. But first we must accept His love.

Why do you think Peter was hesitant to let Christ wash his feet? _____
_____
_____
_____
_____

Have you ever felt this way when someone tried to minister to you? When? Why?
_____
_____
_____
_____
_____

Only through God's great grace and mercy, did Jesus take our death sentence and give us right standing before the holy and righteous God almighty.

God is love. God loves others through us, and God loves us through others.

The sin of pride can come in all kinds of packages. Sometimes it says, "I am not good enough to be served." Or it is that pious attitude of, "I am just here in Christian service to others. I don't need their help." This sounds holy, but what we are really saying is, "Christ's death on the cross was not enough for me." Jesus always taught by example. He served, and He allowed others to serve Him.

Read John 12:1-3. What does Jesus teach about love in this passage? _____
_____
_____
_____

Jesus let Mary wash His feet with oil and dry them with her hair. He loved her enough to let her demonstrate her love for Him, and she experienced an incredible intimacy with her Lord.

What does 1 John 4:7-12 say about God's love in our lives? _____
_____

In John 13:8, what was Jesus' response to Peter? _____
_____
_____
_____

Jesus was stressing to Peter that Peter had to receive love before he could extend it to others.

According to John 13:12-17, why was Jesus doing this? _____
_____
_____
_____
_____

The Greek word translated *blessed* is *makarios*, which means happy, the nature of that which is the highest good.[12]

One Greek word for *love* is *agape,* which means to actively seek the highest good of another.[13]

Do you see any similarities in these two words? _____
_____
_____

If we give and receive God's love, the result will be happiness in our lives. Notice that we are not told to do this only in certain situations or with certain types of people. Love is like forgiveness. We are to extend it and accept it from everyone without exception. Maybe a factor in our happiness is the fact that when we love God's way, there is no dissension or division, and our focus stays on the Lord.

If we give and receive God's love, the result will be happiness in our lives.

Write out what John 3:16 means to you. _____
_____
_____
_____
_____

God's greatest gift to us is love. Our only gift to Him is to love Him, each other, and a lost world with His love. We can't earn it, get cleaned up enough, or look good enough. We just accept it like we accept salvation. This is called grace. Because God made the ultimate sacrifice to love us by sacrificing His only Son for us, Father God understands the sacrifice He is asking us to make to love the unlovely.

Go back to John 13. When Jesus showed the disciples the full extent of His love, He was showing them the purpose of His ministry on earth. He was showing them the end to which all things relate. He got down on His knees in humble servitude to wash feet, an undesirable, dirty, and unlovable part of the body. His action represents exactly how true love touches, caresses, and massages the hurt and pain in order for restoration, refreshing, and healing to take place. It is in this action that we experience closeness, bonding, giving of our time, our hearts, and His love. It is taking people as they are – smelly, dirty, crooked, disfigured, cracked, and bleeding – and ministering to them.

What does Jesus command us to do in John 15:12? _____
_____

According to Luke 6:27-36, are there any exceptions to that command? _____
_____

Put this passage into your own words. _____
_____
_____
_____
_____
_____

Father God realizes how difficult this is.

How does He provide for us to accomplish this goal of loving the unlovely according to Matthew 19:26 and Luke 1:37? _____

_____

_____

_____

Again read John 13:1-30. When Jesus was teaching His disciples about love, where was Judas? He was still there. When Jesus was washing feet, He unconditionally loved and washed the feet of the man He knew would betray Him! Again, He was teaching us by example. We say, *But Lord, You can't understand what this person did to me or You wouldn't ask me to love them.*

Jesus understands perfectly. He hasn't asked us to do anything He has not done already. He commands us to love our enemies and to love those who hurt us. He made no exceptions in His life, and we are not to either.

In Matthew 22:37-39, what does God command us? _____

_____

_____

_____

Read Colossians 3:12-14. When we are clothed in the fruit of the Spirit with forgiveness and love, what is always the result? _____

_____

_____

_____

Can you think of a time when you did not forgive and extend God's love? What was the result? _____

_____

_____

_____

_____

_____

_____

Why do you think this is so? _____

_____

_____

_____

_____

Jesus understands perfectly. He commands us to love our enemies and to love those who hurt us.

Experiencing and extending God's love changes us and everyone around us. It keeps our focus on God and God alone. I had a wise Sunday school teacher who said, "God is love. When we take His love into a circumstance, we take the very essence of God, and therefore, His power." We can bring the power of God into every circumstance by loving others with His love. That is what will change them forever. Beloved, as Christians we are truly power dressing when we, like Jesus in John 13:1, show the full extent of His love.

In John 17:20-26, Jesus explains our mission as His witnesses called to minister reconciliation. Write this passage out in your own words as a prayer and acceptance of the calling to this ministry.

TRUTHS TO EMBRACE

_____

_____

_____

_____

_____

_____

Experiencing and extending God's love changes us and everyone around us.

"God is love. When we take His love into a circumstance, we take the very essence of God, and therefore, His power."

BREAK DOWN THE WALLS

There is no fear in love. But perfect love drives out fear, because fear has to do with punishment. The one who fears is not made perfect in love.

1 John 4:18

Jesus was my only hope for healing and restoration.

I spent the first forty years of my life enslaved to the stronghold of insecurity. I never felt like I measured up or that I fit in. As with any bondage, it only got worse as time went on. I worked very hard at being the best wife, mother, friend, and daughter, only to feel like I always came up short. At night, as I lay in bed, I would go over the things that I did not accomplish. I felt like such a failure. It seemed like everyone else did a better job, was noticed, and had a group of friends to which to belong.

Many issues from my past made me feel this way, but the bottom line is, the fear from my insecurity was immobilizing me. Jesus was my only hope for healing and restoration. I would walk into a room and feel totally out of place. I would sit in a group of friends (like at a Bible study) and feel completely like an outcast. When I was in a group, I felt like a glass wall came up all around me. As a result, I backed away from everyone.

It is devastating to feel this way. The worst part is that while this is going on inside of us, those around us perceive something totally different.

In the midst of all this, I was in leadership at my church and my children's schools, and active in my neighborhood. Most people saw me as an accomplished leader who could handle social obligations and church work, and manage being president of this or that organization, while handling family and home with ease.

The truth was, I was a wreck inside. There were many times that I would call a friend for lunch and if she were busy, I would be so devastated by the rejection that I cried myself to sleep that night.

I prayed for many years for God to heal my insecurity. Then one day, at Bible study, God miraculously did it, and it was the most amazing day of my life! After prayer, I opened my eyes and everything looked different. My whole outlook on life changed.

Several weeks later, I was asked to give my testimony at the ladies' Bible study. When I had finished, a woman I knew casually came up to me with tears streaming down her face. "I never knew what you were going through," she said. "I just thought you were unapproachable!" My fear of not "measuring up," my fear that I did not "fit in," came across to others as my being aloof and unapproachable.

One of our greatest fears is that if people really knew our past (or our present), they would no longer love us.

Read 1 John 4:18, and fill in the blanks.
There is no fear in love. But _____ love _____ out fear.

The word *drive* in this verse is the Greek word *ballo,* which means to throw or let go of a thing, or to give over to one's care.[4] The Greek word translated *perfect* is *teleioo,* which means to make perfect, to complete, to add what is yet wanting in order to render a thing full, or to bring to the end proposed.[5]

God's love is perfect. His love makes us complete. Understanding His love is what we need in order to be full and not wanting for anything or anyone.

What does 2 Corinthians 12:9 say that God's grace is? _____
_____

We can give over our hurts, our insecurities, and our fears because we can entrust them to the care of our Savior. We can rest in His perfect love, knowing all the voids of our lives will be filled by Him because He *is* sufficient. God knows who we are, and He loves us anyway.

For me, the hardest thing to face about my insecurity (which made me seem unapproachable) was realizing the root of the problem. I always saw myself as a "victim." Because I had experienced conditional love and acceptance from friends and family, I had built up walls of protection.

The reality is, insecurity is self-centeredness. It is focusing on myself and how a thing affects "me."

I needed to get my eyes off me and focused on Him. I didn't trust God to take my problem and really heal it. I didn't understand or believe that I could walk boldly into His throne room because my *Abba* loves me. I didn't understand my Father God's love and grace.

Read Hebrews 4:16. What do we receive when we approach the throne of grace with confidence? _____
_____

We can give over our hurts, our insecurities, and our fears because we can entrust them to the care of our Savior. We can rest in His perfect love, knowing all the voids of our lives will be filled by Him because He is sufficient.

If our fear is that love will be withdrawn when our true self is revealed, what we need is grace (unmerited favor) and mercy (getting what we do not deserve — God's love).

In wanting to be a part of the family or group, I was afraid I wasn't working hard enough to earn acceptance. Subconsciously, I believed that if I didn't do everything right, I wouldn't be accepted. I was afraid of being rejected – in fact, I expected it.

Write Romans 8:15 in your own words. _____

_____

_____

_____

_____

_____

I did not understand my *Abba's* passion and compassion for me and His unconditional love that accepts me as I am.

According to Ezekiel 43:27, since Jesus is the ultimate and complete sacrifice for our sins, what does Father God declare? _____

_____

_____

_____

I did not understand that my Father totally forgives me, is ever available, and delights in me. I did not understand that I bring Him great pleasure.

According to Zephaniah 3:17, how does your Father feel about you? _____

_____

_____

_____

_____

According to Acts 10:34 and Ephesians 6:9, I did not understand that Father God understands me, gives me everything, and shows _____.

I did not realize who I was in Christ Jesus.

What does Romans 8:17 say that we are? _____

_____

_____

_____

Read Deuteronomy 31:6. I did not understand that Father God heals my hurts, calms my fears, carries me, and pulls me up on His lap, and that _____

_____.

Most of all, I did not understand that He loved me first, even when I could not love myself. He loved me in my self-centeredness, my unfaithfulness, my pride, and in the depth of my depravity.

Write out 1 John 4:19. _____

_____

Not understanding God's love – that we are His well-loved children – is one of the biggest hindrances to the Christian walk. This lack of understanding feeds our fears, hurts, betrayals, and false perceptions to which we quietly hold. It immobilizes us and steals our joy. It keeps us from participating in the ministry to which God has called us. It causes division among us.

However, Jesus is in the healing business. Jesus can stand in the gap for our parents, our friends, and even our spouses. Our walls of protection not only separate us from others, they also separate us from *God's* healing and love!

According to Romans 5:6-11, Hebrews 9:15, and 1 Peter 3:18, what was the purpose of Christ's death? _____

_____

_____

_____

According to Psalm 25:15, why should you keep your eyes on the Lord? _____

_____

_____

_____

What is one of the biggest snares in your life? _____

_____

_____

_____

Read Psalm 119:33-37. What do you have when your eyes are focused on the Lord? What is your focus when it is on yourself? _____

_____

_____

_____

_____

Not understanding God's love – that we are His well-loved children – is one of the biggest hindrances to the Christian walk.

Jesus is in the healing business.

According to Psalm 145:15, how is Father God sufficient when your eyes are on Him? _____

_____

_____

_____

_____

When our eyes are fixed on our sovereign Lord, we see through His view or opinion.

Read Psalm 141:8-9.

The Hebrew word for *eye* is *ayin*. It means *eye*, but it also refers to mental or spiritual faculties, or one's view or opinion.[16]

When our eyes are fixed on our sovereign Lord, we see through His view or opinion. That completely changes how we perceive things. We no longer look through the stronghold of criticism. We look through eyes of love, grace, and mercy. This changes our whole demeanor, our approachability to the body of Christ, and our ability to be used in ministering reconciliation.

The Hebrew word translated *trust* or *refuge* is *chacah*. It means to seek refuge, to flee for protection, to put trust in, to confide or to hope in.[17] When we take refuge or trust in the Lord instead of our feelings, circumstances, or the opinions of others, we can have confidence in His love, His protection, and His trustworthiness. Only Father God is worthy of our trust, because only He will never disappoint us.

When the psalmist pled not *to be given over* to death, he used the Hebrew word *arah*, meaning to pour out, lay bare, empty, or expose himself.[18]

Isn't that why we put up walls and become unapproachable? We are afraid of being exposed. We think, *If they really knew who I am, or what I think or do, I would be condemned.*

God knows. He loves us anyway and accepts us completely into His family as His children. We have the rights and privileges of children of the King, not because of what we did, but because of what Jesus did. Because we are *Abba's* children, the only thing exposed will be the fact that we belong to Jesus and are saved by grace.

Read 2 Timothy 1:7-9.

We are called to testify of the Lord through our lives. In order to do that, we must focus on Him and look through His eyes of love, grace, and mercy so that we become approachable to others.

What is your focus? What in your life causes you to put up walls? What keeps you from being approachable? _____

_____

_____

_____

Reread 1 John 4:18. Let His perfect love drive out your fears. Remember, the word drive means to give something over to another's care, uncertain about the results.[19] Give your insecurities over to Jesus and trust Him with the results. Write out your prayer in the space below.

TRUTHS TO EMBRACE

_____

_____

_____

_____

_____

_____

_____

_____

_____

TAKE OFF THE MASK

But everything exposed by the light becomes visible, for it is light that makes everything visible.
Ephesians 5:13-14a

One Sunday night after a guest speaker at our church encouraged us to get right with God, one of our men stood up to speak. This member had never spoken out in church before. In fact, there had been a time when his wife and I took our children to church and prayed for our husbands to join us.

At this point, he and his family were active church members and a very close family unit. He was a good husband and a very loving and attentive dad. But that night, when God called him to remove the mask we saw, he obeyed. He said that he had not been the spiritual leader he knew God was calling him to be. He took his wife and children by the hands and led them to the altar to pray. When he did, everything changed. By taking off his mask to be "real" in the body of Christ, God was glorified in ways that I had never dreamed possible when his wife and I had prayed for him.

Read Ephesians 5:13-17.

The way we view others affects the way we either respond or react to them, because the things on which we focus determine our reality.

We know that God is light. The Greek word translated *visible* is *phaneroo*. It means to be realized, to become known, and to thoroughly understand who and what one is.[20]

When we remove our masks and God shines Himself, the light of the world, on our lives and our hearts, we thoroughly understand who and what we are. We realize that we cannot meet the standard set by God almighty, maker of heaven and earth. We realize that we are no different than anyone else – except by the grace of God. This changes how we view ourselves and how we view others. We view things through our Father's eyes and not our own, which too often perceive through strongholds. The way we view others affects the way we either respond or react to them, because the things on which we focus determine our reality.

When we take off our masks, we focus on the Lord Jesus Christ and His righteousness, not our own. When we do this we cannot help but respond to others in love and grace. We give up the hurts and let God heal our hearts. We give up judging others because we know what we are ourselves, apart from the grace of God. Instead, we walk in His love and peace.

According to Matthew 5:48 and 19:16-26, what is the standard to which God is calling us? _____

_____

_____

What are some of the masks we wear so that Christ's light cannot shine to illuminate who and what we are? _____

_____

_____

Most masks are determined by our self-image. They represent the way we want others to perceive us, or the way we perceive ourselves.

Most masks are determined by our self-image. They represent the way we want others to perceive us, or the way we perceive ourselves. When we put on masks of unforgiveness, hurt, pain, greed, selfishness, workaholism, judgment, arrogance, or pride, we become just like actors in costumes portraying someone other than who we really are. Inside we are something totally different, but to the viewer of the performance, we are the character in the costume.

Anyone who has ever watched a clown understands the layers of makeup and clothing, not to mention the change in mindset, it takes to become a different person. You wear a lot of extra "stuff" to present this image. In the spiritual realm, this extra baggage becomes the masks and strongholds through which we see, hear, and react to the world.

When God shines His light on us, He reveals our masquerade. When we finally give Him our costumes and masks, we become approachable children of God who can extend love and grace to all we encounter.

What does Hebrews 12:1 command us to do? _____

_____

_____

According to Hebrews 12:2, where are we to fix our eyes? _____

_____

Is God trying to be mean by asking us to take off our masks? Is this a punishment for wrongdoing? Why would He ask us to do this? Answer these questions by writing Hebrews 12:4-11 in your own words.

_____

_____

_____

_____

_____

_____

What is our major motive for wearing the mask? _____
_____

Fear is the dominant motive for everything in our lives. This word *fear* defined in the Greek language means to be afraid of, to revere, to stand in awe of, or to show honor and reverence for.[21] We either walk in fear of man or in fear of the Lord.

According to Isaiah 51:7, how are we to respond to man's reproach or insults?
_____
_____

We either walk in fear of man or in fear of the Lord.

According to John 12:42-43, what is the opposite of fear? _____
_____

According to Galatians 1:10, can we fear God and man at the same time? _____
_____
_____

According to the following verses, what happens when we fear God?

Psalm 128:1 _____
_____

Psalm 34:9 _____
_____

Job 28:28 _____
_____

Proverbs 16:6 _____
_____

Isaiah 33:6 _____
_____

Isaiah 41:13 _____
_____

Psalm 111:10 _____
_____

In Romans 8:14-17, what does Father God say about us? _____
_____

According to 1 John 5:19, we *know* that we are _____ of God.

Read 1 Peter 1:13-17. Out of holy fear for Father God, as His children, we show honor and reverence by _____.

According to 1 Peter 1:14, what does our life become when either we do not know Jesus or we don't walk in His ways? _____

_____

According to Galatians 5:1, why did Jesus come? _____

_____

Jesus did not come just to give us eternal life; He also came so that we could walk victoriously on earth as His dearly loved children, no longer enslaved to the fears of this world.

Read Philippians 2:12-13.

The working out of our salvation is for His glory and His purpose. The Greek word translated *trembling* is *tromos,* which is used to describe the anxiety of one who distrusts his ability to completely meet all requirements, but who religiously does his utmost to fulfill his duty.[22] When we work out our salvation with fear and trembling, we stand in awe and reverential fear of God almighty, realizing that we cannot trust our own ability to meet His command of being holy or perfect. We religiously do our utmost to fulfill our duty by relying on the grace of God to work in our lives. We trust Him with our lives and give Him our masks so that He can change us. The changes in us and our holy response to situations, people, and suffering are a confirmation to the world that we are children of God.

Basically, we are putting the fact of our salvation, our being Father God's children, to work in our lives as a witness for all to see. We also understand that God causes some things in our lives that are for His glory and therefore our lives' turn of events may not be as we would have chosen for ourselves.

We stand on God's promise in Matthew 19:26. Write it out in your own words.

_____

_____

_____

_____

On the Sunday night when my friend stood up and took off his mask, his life and many other lives in our fellowship changed forever in Christ Jesus. He realized that

The working out of our salvation is for His glory and His purpose.

When we work out our salvation with fear and trembling, we stand in awe and reverential fear of God almighty, realizing that we cannot trust our own ability to meet His command of being holy or perfect.

he could not trust in his own ability to work out his salvation and become the spiritual head of his household that God had called him to be. Only by fear and trembling, by distrusting his own ability and trusting in God's ability could God's call become a reality. From behind his mask, my friend appeared to others to be the perfect husband and father. But God called him to a higher standard, just as He calls each one of us to a higher calling. Our standard is not the world. Our standard is to be perfect as He is perfect, through the grace of God.

By one man's taking off his mask and letting the light shine on exactly who he was, the power of darkness was broken in our fellowship. Others followed his lead and took off their own masks. Prayer and healing took place all over the sanctuary, and we experienced an unprecedented revival in our fellowship. Through that, God was glorified in ways we'd never imagined.

Of what are you afraid? Do you see yourself as a beloved child of God, or are you an actor portraying a role other than who you really are? What is your mask? Through the power of the Father's love, leave it at the foot of the cross and let His love consume you. Write your prayer below.

TRUTHS TO EMBRACE

_____
_____
_____
_____
_____
_____
_____
_____
_____

Week 5

QUIT WAITING FOR THE OTHER GUY

This week we will search the scriptures to discover what God requires of us in order to be His ministers of reconciliation. We will study the examples He gives us through His Word and His actions. He never asks us to do anything that He has not already done. We will learn what we need to begin ministering reconciliation and how this is accomplished. Best of all, we will confirm who we are to our Father God: His beloved children.

DAY 1
Being the "Big Person"

DAY 2
Giving Up

DAY 3
Big Brother

DAY 4
Peace

DAY 5
The Beloved

BEING THE "BIG PERSON"

Therefore, if you are offering your gift at the altar and there remember that your brother has something against you, leave your gift there in front of the altar. First go and be reconciled to your brother: then come and offer your gift.

Matthew 5:23-24

> *Grace is love that stoops down and scoops us up when we are wrong, when we are being unfair, when we are stubborn and unreasonable. Grace is being given what we don't deserve instead of the justice from the law that we do deserve.*

Why do I always have to be the big person? It's a question I've asked God many times. I don't know about you, but it seems to me that I'm the one who always has to make the first move, regardless of whether I am wrong or right. *How unfair!* I have complained to the Lord. He gently reminds me that when I am looking for fairness, I am walking in legalism. I am setting down a list of rules for myself and others to live by, instead of basking in (and extending!) His grace.

Grace is love that stoops down and scoops us up when we are wrong, when we are being unfair, when we are stubborn and unreasonable. Grace is being given what we don't deserve instead of the justice from the law that we do deserve. Extending God's grace is being the "big person."

Read Mark 14:27-31, Luke 22:33, and Matthew. 26:33-35. What does Peter promise Jesus? _____

_____

_____

Peter was very passionate and emphatic in proclaiming his loyalty to the Lord regardless of the others who might "turn back." As I've grown older, I've realized that the things I rashly proclaimed I would never do when I was younger are the very things I have done! The words "never" and "always" are spoken most often from the lips of a legalist believing she is "above everything and capable of nothing."

Have you ever promised anyone that you would never abandon them, only to do exactly that? Have you ever felt betrayed by someone that you thought would never leave you or hurt you? Have you been in a situation where you felt totally alone because none of your friends or family stood by you when you needed them most? What were your expectations for that situation? How were they not met?

_____

_____

_____

According to Matthew 26:31 and Mark 14:30, did Jesus expect Peter (or us) to never fail Him? Did Jesus put His trust in Peter or any of His disciples to carry Him through His trials? _____

_____

_____

According to Mark 14:38, why not? _____

_____

Read Luke 22:39-43. Who did Jesus expect to comfort Him and to carry Him through His trials? _____

_____

_____

Was it out of the ordinary for Jesus to go off by Himself at this place to pray to His Father? Why or why not? _____

_____

Where is your usual place to turn when you are facing trials? _____

_____

For most of my life, I have looked to my friends to help me face my trials, only to find they were not enough. Only God is *big enough* to be there for me without exception or disappointment.

List the captives you need to set free from being "big enough" for you.

_____

Why do Luke 4:18 and Isaiah 61:1 say that Jesus came? _____

_____

When you hold someone captive to meet your expectations, it not only imprisons *them*, but it also keeps you locked up. You become a jailer who is always on duty, ensuring that the prisoner remains locked up.

Read Isaiah 45:13. Do you have to pay a price or meet a certain standard for Christ to set you or your prisoners free? Will you let Him set you and your "captives" free today, and turn to Him knowing that He alone is big enough to save you?

_____

_____

_____

_____

It is a good thing that Jesus did not put His hopes in Peter to stand by Him at all times. According to Mark 14:66-71, what happened? _____
_____
_____

Was Peter as passionate about his denial as he was about his previous promise? How do you know? _____
_____
_____

What does that tell you about our promises and good intentions? _____
_____
_____

Read John 21:1-19.

What did Peter decide to do? _____
_____

What effect did it have on the other disciples? _____
_____

When we are at odds with someone or are disappointed in others or ourselves, we sometimes feel the need to go back to something from our past that is comfortable or just an old habit. This is especially true if we have tried something new and failed. Peter was a fisherman. He knew that he had turned away from the Lord, from when he had vehemently promised Him, in front of his friends, that he would be loyal to Him regardless of what anyone else did. He must have felt like an unworthy failure.

Read John 1:35-42. What did Jesus call Simon? _____
_____

The name "Peter" is the Greek word *petros* meaning "a piece of rock."[1]

What did Jesus promise Peter in Matthew 16:18-19? _____
_____

Do you think that Peter thought he could no longer be a rock God would use, since he had turned away from Christ during His trial? _____
_____
_____

Have you ever felt that way? _____

_____

Have you ever felt that way about a friend? After they hurt you or failed you, how did your expectations of them change? _____

_____

_____

How do you think Jesus would have responded in the same situation? _____

_____

_____

Write out Matthew 5:23-24. _____

_____

_____

_____

_____

_____

The key phrase in this verse is *has something against you*. Jesus is calling us to reconcile both when we are right, and when we are wrong. Being the "big person" can mean going to someone when they are upset with you and you have done nothing wrong. It can also mean going to someone when you were wrong and they were right. The common thread between both of these scenarios is that we are *always* called to go to them.

Jesus is calling us to reconcile both when we are right, and when we are wrong.

"Going" can be a difficult command to obey. Have you ever thought, *But Lord, You don't understand how much they hurt me. I didn't do anything to them to deserve that treatment.* What had Jesus done to Peter to deserve Peter's turning his back on Him when Jesus was being tried and crucified?

Read John 21.

In verse 5 how did Jesus address Peter and the other disciples? _____

_____

In verse 6, Jesus said for them to throw their nets on the right side of the boat in order to catch fish. What had Jesus promised Peter in Mark 1:16-18?

_____

_____

_____

Do you wonder if, as Peter fished, he thought with disappointment that now he would only be a fisherman instead of a fisher of men for Christ? _____

_____

_____

Read John 21:15-19. What do you think Jesus was trying to do?_____

_____

_____

Jesus had already reconciled Peter's sin when He died on the cross. Now He was reconciling His friendship with Peter and reinstating him as a leader among the disciples. Peter denied Jesus three times. In his reconciliation, Jesus asked him the same question three times. It took that long for Peter to finally understand. Jesus is always patient with us as He lovingly brings us back into fellowship with Himself. *Jesus was being the big person with Peter!*

As ministers of reconciliation, we are called to "reinstate" those who have turned away from us or let us down.

Through his encounter with Christ, the guilt that imprisoned Peter was gone! He had been forgiven once and for all. Not only did Christ's redemptive grace wash away his shame, but the questions Jesus asked him revealed the truth about Peter's love for Christ.

As ministers of reconciliation, we are called to "reinstate" those who have turned away from us or let us down. We may confront them, as Jesus did with Peter, or we may simply love them unconditionally. The Holy Spirit gives us direction for every instance in our lives. Either way, unconditional love and forgiveness is not an option for believers. Only God is big enough to be enough for those times when we want to hold others captive to our expectations.

Do you need to settle a pride issue with the Lord? When you refuse to be the big person who extends His grace, you usually have a problem with pride. Being the "big person" means laying down your pride, and being willing to let your captives go free and love them with the same unconditional love and forgiveness that Jesus gives you.

TRUTHS TO EMBRACE

_____

_____

_____

_____

_____

_____

GIVING UP

Therefore, I urge you, brothers, in view of God's mercy, to offer your bodies as living sacrifices, holy and pleasing to God – this is your spiritual act of worship.

Romans 12:1

The biggest hindrance to a life abandoned to Christ Jesus is self-centeredness. Self-centeredness is about personal desires, personal passions, and personally perceived needs and wants. The issue always goes back to "me" and how "I" am affected, instead of what would glorify the Lord. I know firsthand, because in my flesh, I am a very self-centered person. I don't want to be the big person because of how it affects me. I have trouble with forgiveness when my feelings have been hurt. I don't extend mercy because of what was done to me. I can't say no because it might affect the way someone views me. I don't want to expose my conviction of sin because it might make me look bad. The list goes on and on.

Throughout my life, I have abandoned myself to a variety of things, (by abandoned, I mean focused on), and my focus has changed as I have moved from one phase of life to another. God was always there, but He wasn't always in the forefront. In high school, my focus was on boys and making the drill team. In college, my focus was on dating Bruce, making good grades, and having fun. After graduation, Bruce and I married, and my home and marriage became my focus. For a while, I focused on my job, and then buying and remodeling my first house. After my son was born, my focus became my children. There have been times of focus on the PTA, car pools, and taking care of elderly grandparents. All of these things may seem honorable, but too often they became my main focus. Then there were those times when my focus was on my anger, disappointment, or self-pity. Too often, it seems each new day brings with it a new passion and new direction. When we allow the focal point of our priorities to be anything other than Jesus, there will be no joy, no peace, and worst of all, no glorifying God in our lives.

Total abandonment to our holy God is the key to being the "big person." It is the unselfish devotion of a love that is seeking the highest good of our Father in heaven. We must come to a place where our total focus is to bring glory to God, where nothing else matters except His will being done. This is the exact opposite of what the world tells us. The world tells us to take care of ourselves first because no one else will. The world tells us to do unto others as they do to you – or *before* they do unto you. On the surface, abandonment seems too hard; but in reality it is not. Once we finally give up and let God take over, the pressure is off.

Total abandonment to our holy God is the key to being the "big person." It is the unselfish devotion of a love that is seeking the highest good of our Father in heaven.

What are some of the things to which you have abandoned your own life? _____

_____

_____

We are very quick to point our fingers at someone who has committed adultery. In the church, we too often consider this one of the "big" sins. We give lip service to forgiveness, yet all the while, we are standing ready to enforce the consequences. We piously wonder how someone could give their body and heart to someone outside of their marriage, when they had made a covenant before God to love, honor, and adore their spouse and none other.

Read John 8:2-11. How did Jesus differentiate adultery from other sins? _____

_____

_____

_____

What is your definition of adultery? _____

_____

_____

When we abandon ourselves to anything or anyone other than God, we commit spiritual adultery.

When we abandon ourselves to anything or anyone other than God, we commit spiritual adultery. That is why no one in that passage could cast the first stone; everyone had committed adultery before a holy God.

It sickens me to think of all the times that I have loved another by giving myself to a cause, an opportunity, a church committee, and so on, above my love for God.

The reason we don't want to be the "big" person like Jesus is because our hearts are not totally given to our heavenly Father. We come home to the Lord and give Him our everything, but then the next day we flirt with sin. We love our flesh, our self-centeredness, our insecurity, our jobs, our image, our righteous indignation, our church work, our children, or whatever else is above God for that minute, that hour, that day. Then we must face the reality that we have committed adultery against our Bridegroom, Jesus. We can't throw any stones because we are no better.

During the conversation with the Pharisees and the woman, what was Jesus doing?

_____

_____

Exodus 34:1 tells us the only other time that God wrote something. What did He write? _____

_____

_____

We don't know exactly what Jesus was writing on the ground, but it must have been significant. Scripture records God and Jesus writing only twice. One was to give us the law, and I believe the other was to give us grace.

What does Romans 3:10 tell us? _____

_____

We are all hopeless without the mercy of God's grace. Praise God that as Christians we have hope in Jesus Christ.

How do we know this, according to the following verses?

1 Peter 1:3-5 _____

_____

Ephesians 2:1-9 _____

_____

Write out Romans 12:1. _____

_____

_____

The phrase *in view* (or *by*) is translated from the Greek word *dia*, meaning the ground or reason by which something is or is not done.[2] The reason we offer our bodies as living sacrifices, holy and pleasing to God, is His great mercy to us.

List how God has been merciful to you. _____

_____

Because of God's mercy, we offer our bodies as living sacrifices.

Because of God's mercy, we offer our bodies as living sacrifices (something we do while we are here on earth). We don't just ask Jesus to be our Savior and then wait until heaven to commit ourselves fully to Him. The way we live, think, and feel is to be a living sacrifice, holy and pleasing to God.

The word translated in the NIV as *spiritual* is the Greek word *logikos*.[3] The *King James Version* translates the word as *reasonable*. I prefer that translation. The meaning in the original Greek is that the sacrifice is service to God which is to be through intelligent meditation or reflection, in contrast to those offered by thoughtless habit, ritual, or compulsion.[4] In other words, the presentation of our bodies, our very lives, is to be in accordance with the spiritual intelligence of those who are new creatures in Christ and are mindful of "the mercies of God." On the surface, *spiritual* sounds good, but when we truly understand God's mercy, the only *reasonable* thing we can do is offer ourselves as a living sacrifice. It is a natural response. There is nothing too great to offer unto our Lord in view of His mercy to us. Our reasonable act of worship is not something that we do because we have to or because we should. When we realize what Jesus did for us in our sin and total unworthiness, we are compelled by our awareness of Father God's great mercy toward us. What He asks of us is so insignificant compared to what He did for us at Calvary.

Yesterday, we studied Peter, the rock. Once Peter finally grasped the love of God and became rooted and grounded in it, he truly became a rock on which Jesus could build His church. His was a life totally abandoned to Christ because he understood God's love and mercy. In view of all this, he daily abandoned his life, his will, his fears, and his desires as his reasonable act of worship.

In Isaiah 61:3, what does the Word say we will be called? _____
_____

Why? _____

I live in the country with lots of oak and pine trees. When storms come, I love to look out at the trees. The pine trees sway back and forth in the wind. They are better protected if they are planted in a group. A lone pine tree is in greater danger of breaking than a group of pines. Sometimes they just snap in two, if the storm is too severe. Also, the oak trees stand firm in the storms. Their root systems are strong and well established, so they can stand alone no matter how great the storm. Sometimes dead or damaged limbs break off, but the tree still stands firmly rooted.

According to Ephesians 3:14-19, when we are rooted and established in love, what do we have the power to do? _____
_____
_____

When we understand Father God's love, it captures our heart, soul, and mind. As our reasonable act of worship, we want to surrender everything because of His love and mercy. We become willing prisoners of His love. We are all prisoners of something: you can either be a prisoner of sin or of grace. The choice is yours.

Read 2 Peter 2:19. Of what are you a prisoner? _____

What is the fruit, or outcome, of that? _____
_____

What does Ephesians 4:1-2 tell us that prisoners of God's love are to do? _____
_____
_____

Because of God's great mercy to us, as our reasonable act of worship, we are called to be the "big person" and to glorify Him by being completely humble and gentle; patient and _____

in love. The fruit of this will be unity of the Spirit through the bond of peace.

What does 2 Chronicles 16:9 say that the Lord wants to do to those whose hearts are fully committed to Him? _____

_____

According to Joshua 3, when we consecrate, or abandon, ourselves to the Lord, what will He do? _____

_____

_____

When you abandon yourself to the Lord, you can stand firm while the river rages all around you. I challenge you today to repent of your adulterous ways. By repent, I mean to turn from adultery to God. Give yourself completely to your Bridegroom, Jesus. In view of God's mercy, offer your body as a living sacrifice, holy and pleasing to God – it's your reasonable act of worship.

TRUTHS TO EMBRACE

_____

_____

_____

_____

_____

_____

BIG BROTHER

Do not conform any longer to the pattern of this world, but be transformed by the renewing of your mind.

Romans 12:2

A mind is a terrible thing to waste.

A mind is a terrible thing to waste. I am appalled at the things on which I have wasted my own mind. It is another stumbling block to my being the "big person." Whatever my mind is fixed on is the thing to which I am faithful.

Do you find yourself thinking the same things over and over, almost as if you have a tape player in your mind? You may have a problem with someone, or they may say something that hurts you, and you play the conversation over and over in your head. Then you plan what you would like to say to them, and the tape starts up again. You might even have an argument or confrontation with that person in your head, and you can experience the same emotion, hurt, and anger as you would in reality. These things put you in a bad mood, making you depressed or angry.

Playing these tapes are a real waste of my mind. They stimulate my emotions and take my focus off the Lord. I become susceptible to the wiles of Satan instead of focused on the glorification of my God. It is like the hamster running on the wheel, not knowing how to get off. Praise God that His Word addresses our sin. The first step is to admit this is sin in our life, repent, and give it to God. The next step is found in Romans 12.

Write out Romans 12:2. _____

_____

_____

_____

According to Matthew 16:23, when I have my mind on the things of man instead of the things of God, what is caused in my life (and in the lives of others)?

_____

_____

According to Matthew 22:37-38, what is God's greatest command to us?

_____

_____

Read Deuteronomy 28:15-28. What can happen to our minds when we disobey God's commands? _____

_____

_____

According to Matthew 6:22-23, how do our eyes affect our whole bodies? _____

_____

_____

What does Romans 12:2 promise us we will be able to do if we are transformed by the renewing of our minds? _____

_____

_____

The Greek word for *renewal* is translated *anakainosis*. It means a daily renewal where there is an adjustment of the moral and spiritual vision and thinking to the mind of God.[5] The Greek word translated *mind* is *nous,* meaning a particular mode of thinking and judging.[6] The renewal of our minds is not a one-time event but a daily choice. For me, I need to start every morning asking God to renew my mind and give me His eyes with which to see and His ears with which to hear. Often the reason that I can't be the "big person" is because I see through my own eyes and not His, so I am judgmental, jealous, and confused. Father God must be my stronghold or something else will.

The renewal of our minds is not a one-time event but a daily choice.

According to Exodus 34:14, when something other than God is our stronghold, how does He respond? _____

_____

Who does Deuteronomy 4:24 say that God is? _____

_____

How does God feel toward us according to the following verses?

> • *Then will the* LORD *be jealous* _____ *his land, and pity his people. (Joel 2:18 KJV)*
> • *So the angel that communed with me said unto me, Cry thou, saying, Thus saith the* LORD *of hosts; I am jealous* _____ *Jerusalem and _____ Zion with a great jealousy. (Zechariah 1:14 KJV)*

What does it mean to be jealous *for* someone? _____

_____

_____

_____

What is the difference between being jealous *for* someone and being jealous *of* someone? _____

_____

We are in a spiritual battle,

and most of it takes place

in our minds.

God is jealous *for* us. He desires our total devotion and the daily renewal of our minds to His will, because He knows it is for our own good.

In 2 Corinthians 11:2-3, why did Paul say he was jealous for the Corinthians? What would happen to their minds if they were not renewed daily? _____

_____

_____

We are in a spiritual battle, and most of it takes place in our minds. I don't think that I have ever outwardly committed a sin that was not first conceived in my mind. We are at war with Satan to keep our minds faithful to God our Father.

Write out 2 Corinthians 10:3-5. _____

_____

_____

_____

_____

_____

_____

_____

Now let's take a look at how our *Abba* handles the situation when someone hurts or wrongs Him.

What does Psalm 103:11-13 say the Father has done with our sin? _____

_____

Read Luke 15:11-32. This is a story of two brothers and their *Abba* (Daddy). What did the younger brother do in verses 11-16? _____

_____

_____

Land was very important in the Jewish culture because it was handed down from generation to generation. In this story, the younger brother didn't just pack a bag and leave home; he sold off his part of the family estate for money and then squandered the money in his new wild lifestyle.

How do you think this made his older brother and father feel? _____

_____

What does verse 17 tell us happened to the younger brother? _____

_____

What did he do next? _____

_____

I love the way his father responded to him (verses 20-24). This is a perfect picture of how our *Abba* responds to us – without exception.

When did his father first notice him? _____

Your heavenly Father is always watching for you.

What did his father do next? _____

_____

What did the son have to do before his father came to him? _____

_____

In verses 22-24, describe the father's heart for his son. What was his desire and his will? What was the focus in his mind? _____

_____

_____

_____

The father extended love and mercy to his son before the son repented.

We see here a beautiful picture of forgiveness. The father extended love and mercy to his son *before* the son repented. His father ran to his son even though his son had been in the wrong. The son later apologized and repented. The father not only reconciled their relationship, out of his great love and mercy, he also reconciled his son to everyone around by restoring his position and authority in the family. The kindness of the father was based on his love and mercy – not on the son's behavior or accomplishments. However, the family was not totally reconciled because the older brother was holding some major grudges. He had probably rehearsed several different scenarios regarding his wayward brother, and likely none of them included grace and mercy.

According to verse 28, how did the older brother react? _____

_____

Was he jealous *for* or *of* his younger brother? _____

_____

_____

Yet, what did his father do with the older brother? _____

_____

I love that no matter whether we are the older or younger brother, our *Abba* never waits for us to get cleaned up and come crawling to Him. He comes to us. Beloved, how many times have you been wronged and out of righteous indignation stood firm, your arms crossed and your feet tapping waiting for the other person to apologize? God calls us to be the "big person" and extend His love and mercy, just as He has done for us. God leads us with Jesus as our example.

Read verses 28-30. Where was the older brother's focus? Do you think that he lived a life transformed by the renewing of his mind, or did he conform to the pattern of the world? How did this affect his life, his witness, and his joy? Explain.

_____

_____

_____

_____

Reconciliation is all about God, His glory, and His will.

Has there ever been a time in your life when you have been the older brother? When? _____

_____

_____

Reconciliation is all about God, His glory, and His will. It is understanding God's mercy and offering your body as a living sacrifice, holy and pleasing to God as your reasonable act of worship. It is not living as the world tells us you you have a right to live, because you have sacrificed your rights and your feelings in view of God's mercy. It is being transformed by the renewing of your mind so that you see through His eyes, with His agenda, and with His heart. It is being the "big person" when you have been wronged or hurt because you are faithful to His will and want Him and Him alone to be glorified. Then, like the father, when you come face to face with that person you are angry with, disappointed by, or hurt by, you will have no choice but to reach out in love and mercy before they make the first move. It is not easy, yet in reality, it is harder *not* to do God's will because of the turmoil that causes within. When you come face to face with this situation, stand on God's promise in Luke 15:31-32.

Write out Luke 15:31-32 using your name instead of the words "my son," "you," and "yours." _____

_____

_____

_____

_____

Has your focus become more faithful to someone or a situation other than Father God? He is jealous for you because He loves you and is actively seeking your highest good. Place whatever has drawn away your focus on His altar and ask Him to renew your mind.

```
┌─────────────────────────────────────────────────────┐
│                TRUTHS TO EMBRACE                      │
│  _____  │
│  _____  │
│  _____  │
│  _____  │
│  _____  │
└─────────────────────────────────────────────────────┘
```

PEACE

Peace I leave with you; My peace I give you…

John 14:27

Holy Father,

Oh, to come face to face yesterday with the fact that I was not at peace with You. I have been fighting You off and on for most of my life. Oh, there were times of greatness, but so overshadowed by the more often times of rebellion and struggle. There can be no peace in my life, or with others, until there is true peace with You. I lay down the boxing gloves at Your feet as my sacrificial act of worship. I give up. I give in. I can do that because I know You and know that I can trust You. You are righteous and true and all-knowing. Your love consumes me. I guess it is dying to self. It doesn't matter what I want or think I need. It only matters what You want, Your desires, and You will take care of my real needs. The amazing thing is how, without saying a word after giving up, my friend noticed a difference in me. PEACE! It is incredible. To be in harmony with You put my life in harmony everywhere. Even if it doesn't seem so to the world, the harmony and peace within makes dealing with pressure, hurts, and conflict okay because of the peace from You. It's that verse that says, "Peace I give to you, not as the world does." It is rest and secure borders. I am able to abandon because nothing else matters or compares to peace with You. I praise You for only You are holy. I praise You for only You are good. I praise You because only You are trustworthy and true, righteous and honorable, loving and caring, protecting and sovereign. You are the Alpha and the Omega, almighty God, my Lord, my Savior and my Father.

This was an entry from one of my prayer journals. A friend of mine kept saying that she was not seeing joy in my life. It was humbling to face the fact that my joy was not consistent because I was not at peace with God. I would have those times of total abandonment when I would cry out from my heart, *Whatever, Lord. My life is Yours to use as You choose to glorify Yourself.* Then when the call came in an unexpected way, I would hesitate. *Lord, surely You can't mean this?* And I would begin to whine and pull back.

Writing this Bible study has been one of the most wonderful and most difficult times of my life. Besides the obvious refining fire I walk through as God teaches me the material and implements it in my life, it also involves being pulled aside to sit at His feet. Until now, He has removed everything and everyone from my life to keep my distractions to a minimum, but I am a very social person. I began to whine and complain about being lonely and then I would feel guilty because I wasn't letting God be enough. There was no peace in my life because I was battling God about the thing to which He had called me. Did I really mean the words, *Whatever, Lord,* when I said them? It was time to walk the talk. Time to reconcile and quit fighting. Time to return to the peace of the Father.

The bottom line is that there can be no reconciliation with anything or anyone else in my life unless there is peace with God first.

Read Jonah 1:1-17.

What was Jonah's focus?_____

How did this affect his life?_____

How did this affect the lives of those around him? _____
_____

Was Jonah living a life that glorified God? _____
_____

What did Jonah do in chapter 2?_____

After Jonah made peace with God, how did he respond differently the next time God called (Jonah 3:1-3)? _____
_____

Read Jonah 3:4-10. How were the Ninevites' lives changed? _____
_____
_____

I am greatly convicted when I read this passage. Because of Jonah's disobedience and lack of peace with God, an entire ship of sailors almost missed the grace of God, and an entire city almost faced God's destruction. Jonah, like you and I on occasion, had his eyes focused in the wrong direction. In his self-centeredness, God's will and God's glory were pushed aside. But our Father is sovereign and always faithful.

Jonah, like you and I on occasion, had his eyes focused in the wrong direction.

In His great mercy, what did the Father God do in Jonah 1:17? _____

_____

Has your Father ever provided a fish to swallow you in your disobedience to keep you from drowning in your sin? _____

_____

_____

Read Jonah 4.

Jonah had not totally come to peace with God in this issue.

Was Jonah looking at the Ninevites through a renewed mind? Why or why not?

_____

_____

Only God almighty sees the big picture.

Often, when Father God calls us to do something, we do not understand all of the ramifications of the call. Only God almighty sees the big picture. We must also understand that our lives are to praise and glorify Him and Him alone. Only through His peace are we able to put our hopes, our desires, and our feelings aside for His will and His glory.

I don't want to be like Jonah and risk one person missing the grace of God because of my self-centeredness and lack of faithfulness. I must trust God because I will not always be able to understand why.

What does Isaiah 55:9 teach us? _____

What are we commanded to do in Hebrews 12:14-15? Why? _____

_____

_____

When there is a lack of reconciliation in our lives either with God or with someone or some thing, we are allowing that bitter root to take hold and grow. It will affect those around us. We are always a witness. We can either witness to the glory of God's grace in our life and draw others to Him, or we can witness of our self-centeredness, which lacks peace and drags others away from God. Why would anyone want to be a Christian if there were nothing different about us? If we lack joy and peace, if we are whiny and bitter, if we are fighting among ourselves, then who needs what we have?

Is there a bitter root in your life? If so, what is it? Ask God to reveal it to you and then pull it out. _____

_____

_____

_____

According to 2 Corinthians 13:11 and Isaiah 26:3, what is the prerequisite to peace?

_____

_____

_____

Put Colossians 3:12-15 into your own words. _____

_____

_____

_____

From where does 2 Thessalonians 3:16 tell us our peace comes? _____

_____

_____

Read Philippians 4:4-9.

The word translated here as *anxious* means to be pulled in two directions at one time.[9] That is the opposite of peace. Scripture tells us that when we are anxious, we must take whatever it is and present it to God in prayer. When we truly give it over to Him, the result is peace. However, when we give it to God, we must also give Him the solution. It is our *Whatever, Lord.* There is no peace when we come to God and say, *I want You to resolve this my way.* Why? Because God's ways are higher than our ways; the purpose of our lives is to glorify God, not just to justify ourselves or get our own ways.

In verse 7 the Greek word translated *guard* is *phrourea.* It is a military term meaning to hem in or protect.[8] This protection is by a military guard to either prevent a hostile invasion or to keep the inhabitants of a besieged city from flight. When the peace of God guards our hearts and minds in Christ Jesus, He guards us from satanic attack and from ourselves.

What does this verse mean to you? _____

_____

_____

Because God's ways are higher than our ways; the purpose of our lives is to glorify God, not just to justify ourselves or get our own ways.

Write out Philippians 4:9. _____

_____

_____

_____

_____

_____

It is time to make a renewed mind a lifestyle and not just a habit. You can get out of the habit of doing something quicker than you can form that habit. Scripture promises that if a renewed mind is your lifestyle, the peace of God will be with you.

Today, I challenge you to either make a lifestyle commitment for the first time, or renew your commitment that has faltered. Abandon your life totally to the will of God. Become faithful to a lifestyle governed by a renewed mind in Christ Jesus, not habit. Ask God to do whatever it takes to make yours a life of holiness that glorifies Him, so that everyone who sees you will see the Lord; no one will miss the grace of God; and no bitter root will grow up to cause trouble.

TRUTHS TO EMBRACE

_____

_____

_____

_____

_____

_____

THE BELOVED

For you did not receive a spirit that makes you a slave again to fear, but you received the Spirit of sonship.

Romans 8:15

When one of my sons asked me to help him with a paper he was writing on the correlation between rape and teen violence, I was amazed at the high percentage of violent teens who had experienced a violent childhood. According to research, many act out what they have experienced, either because that is all they know or because it is a way for them to finally be in control. Their self-image is one of hatred and inferiority.

Many times we treat people the way we have been treated. It is a learned response.

Many times we treat people the way we have been treated. It is a learned response.

Today, my prayer is that we will learn a new response – not just how to be a good person who treats people nicely, but what it means to be "in the beloved."

Two very similar words for *beloved* are used in both the Old and New Testament. They are the Hebrew word, '*ahebh,* and the Greek word, *agapao.* It is God's love for His chosen based on respect, a benevolent regard and not an emotion. It means esteemed, dear, favorite, precious, and worthy of respect. The term *beloved* portrays God's tender love for His people, and His infinite affection for Jesus, His "beloved Son." It is used in a similar manner as the Greek word, *agape,* meaning *love.* We are Father God's beloved children based on His choice, an act of His will, not based on emotion, performance, circumstance, or our behavior. We are His beloved children based on His grace and mercy.

When I was five days old, I was adopted into my family. My birth mother, the parents who raised me, and the courts made a contract, a covenant that changed my parentage and family status. For the first five days of my life, I was legally the child of my birth mother, but after that contract, or covenant, was signed, I became the child of my adoptive parents forever.

This contract was not based on my merit or performance; I was just a newborn baby. Nobody knew what I would be like or what my personality or talents were. I was adopted simply because my birth mother was willing to make the sacrifice to put my needs ahead of her own desires.

She knew that she was not in a position to care for me, and she wanted me to have parents who desired a child. As my natural parent, she had the option of keeping me or giving me away. She was not under any binding legal contract to raise me.

My adoptive parents do not have the same options. When they signed the papers to adopt me, they signed an irrevocable contract. Because of the terms of the contract, legally, they can never disown me or give me away. Nothing I say or do, and nothing they say or do can ever change the fact that I am their daughter. We can be mad, sad, happy, or never speak or see each other again, but the legal fact remains that I am their daughter and they are my parents.

Beloved, your Father God made an irrevocable covenant with you. Because Jesus was willing to put your needs ahead of His own desires, He was crucified on the cross for your sins. When you accepted Jesus as your Lord and Savior, you became a beloved child of God based on Father God's covenant with Abraham. This covenant is based on Father God's desire to have you as His child, totally apart from your merit or performance. It is not based on your personality or talents. You are simply adopted into the family of God as His beloved child, and nothing you say or do can ever change that fact. You are His child. He cannot change His mind. It is permanent and everlasting, based completely on God's abundant grace and mercy.

When you accepted Jesus as your Lord and Savior, you became a beloved child of God based on Father God's covenant with Abraham.

Write Galatians 3:23-25 in your own words. _____
_____
_____
_____

According to Romans 4:16-17, how were we adopted into the promise to Abraham's offspring? _____
_____
_____

According to Romans 9:8, does God have two families, His natural children and His adopted children? _____
_____
_____
_____

According to Romans 2:11 and 9:16, is there something you can do to earn more love from God? _____
_____
_____

Write out 1 John 3:1 using your name. Then read it out loud. This is a critical concept to understand, and you need to hear it from your own lips._____

_____

_____

_____

_____

I love the way the NIV uses an exclamation mark to emphasize God's enthusiastic love for His children. The word translated *called* means to call out loud or utter in a loud voice.[9] Your Father God is not ashamed to call you His child before all creation. God is delighted to call our names out loud. In fact, He shouts with joy even though we are ungrateful.

Your Father God is not ashamed to call you His child before all creation.

According to 1 John 3:20 and 4:16, how can He do this? _____

_____

Beloved, God is love, and His love is greater than our evil hearts. His love for us is a choice – His choice.

What do we know according to John 15:16 and 1 Thessalonians 1:4? _____

_____

_____

Can anything change that? Why? See Hebrews 13:5 and John 10:28. _____

_____

_____

_____

_____

_____

As His beloved children, we are heirs to everything in Christ Jesus, and we are on intimate terms with Him. Our Father desires intimacy with us.

According to Galatians 4:5-7 and Romans 8:15, what can we call God almighty, creator of the universe?

_____

_____

As we learned earlier, *Abba* means Daddy. It is a precious term of endearment and extreme closeness used by a child for their father. It exemplifies a very close relationship without restriction. As God's beloved child, I have the right to crawl up in my heavenly Father's lap and put my head against His chest with His loving arms wrapped around me. Have you been there? It is the most wonderful, safest, most

As God's beloved child, I have the right to crawl up in my heavenly Father's lap and put my head against His chest with His loving arms wrapped around me.

secure, and loving place you will ever experience. Your *Abba* longs for you. If you are too weak to climb up, He will pick you up and draw you to Himself. He loves you. You are His favorite! You are His precious child.

When my son, Carl, was a baby, he loved for me to rock him and sing to him. He was often sick as a toddler, and his crying would wake me in the middle of the night. When I got to his room, he would be standing in his crib with his arms stretched out to me saying, "Rock a baby. Rock-a-bye baby."

Not once, no matter how tired I was, did I say, "Leave me alone and go back to sleep!" Of course not! My heart was broken with love for him as I scooped him up and went to our rocking chair where I held him close, dried his tears, sang, and rejoiced over my precious, beloved child until he fell asleep, safe and secure in my arms.

That is what your *Abba* desires from you. He loves you even when you are dirty, at inconvenient times, in the midst of your rebellion, and in disobedience. He just loves you. You are His favorite. You are His precious, beloved child, and when you truly believe that, it changes everything about you.

According to Ephesians 4:1-6, 22-24, and 5:1-7, as His beloved children, what should be different about us? _____

_____

_____

_____

How does Jesus' disciple, John, refer to himself in the following verses?

John 13:23 _____

John 19:26_____

John 20:2_____

John 21:20_____

Do you think John had any doubts about his position in Christ? _____
_____

Do you have any doubts about your belovedness in Christ? _____
_____

According to John 13:23, where was John at the Last Supper? _____
_____

Do you think he worried what the other disciples would think if he reclined against the Lord? Do you think he thought he could do that only if he had "been good" that day? _____
_____
_____

When was the last time you reclined against the Lord? _____
_____
_____

Where was John when Jesus was praying in the Garden of Gethsemane (Mark 14:32-33)? _____
_____
_____

According to John 18:15-16, where was John when Jesus was being tried? _____
_____
_____

(No one knows for sure that the "other disciple" was John, but we believe that it was because this story was included in the book he authored and he always refers to himself as "the disciple" but named everyone else.)

Where was John when Jesus was crucified (John 19:25-26)? _____
_____
_____

Was any other disciple present?_____

Where was John the morning of the resurrection (John 20:1-8)? _____
_____
_____

Where was John when Peter was reconciled to the disciples and Jesus (John 21:20-21)? _____
_____
_____

Because of his close walk with Christ, what was John able to do (John 21:24-25)?

_____

_____

_____

John, more than any of the other disciples, understood what it meant to be the Lord's beloved child. He was secure in the fact that Jesus loved him no matter what.

John, more than any of the other disciples, understood what it meant to be the Lord's beloved child. He was secure in the fact that Jesus loved him no matter what. He was also secure in the fact of the completeness of the love of Christ Jesus. Because of that he freely returned that love and extended it to others. At the cross, Jesus asked John to care for His mother because He knew John so clearly accepted and understood Jesus' love that he could extend that same love to Jesus' mother in her grief. Only John was so abandoned to Christ that he would take the risk to stand by Jesus at the trial and crucifixion. Because John knew he was Jesus' beloved child, nothing was more important to him than the needs and glory of Christ. John's love was not a love of convenience; it was a deliberate choice.

This week we have pondered what it means to be the "big person," and why we, as Christians, always have to make that sacrifice. We make that sacrifice as a deliberate choice, out of our love for our Lord. It is a sacrificial act of worship on our part, not because we are "super-spiritual," but because we are His beloved children.

Write out John 3:16. _____

_____

_____

If God would sacrifice His only Son for our salvation, then why would He require less of us? _____

_____

_____

_____

Read Romans 12:1-2 below.

> *Therefore, I urge you, brothers, in view of God's mercy, to offer your bodies as living sacrifices, holy and pleasing to God – this is your spiritual act of worship. Do not conform any longer to the pattern of this world, but be transformed by the renewing of your mind. Then you will be able to test and approve what God's will is – his good, pleasing and perfect will.*

It is my reasonable act of worship to be the "big person," because I am my *Abba's* beloved child and because I understand the depth of His love and mercy. It is my only reasonable response to love others with the same love that my Father lavishes on me. When someone is cruel, disrespectful, or sarcastic to me, my reasonable act of worship is to love that person with the love of my Father. I am taught love, grace, and mercy from my *Abba*; I then respond to others with what I know. It is a learned response.

If someone I see is acting in disobedience and sin, as God's beloved child I want to respond to them with the same unconditional love that my Father has lavished on me because in reality, I am no better than they are. First Peter 4:8 teaches us, *"love covers over a multitude of sins."* This means that I choose to replace my judgmentalism, my attitudes, and my pride with love and mercy for others. I understand that even though I don't deserve it, I am my Father's beloved child, and He is not ashamed of me. He shouts it loudly in the heavenlies. Who am I to do anything less?

We should be known for being the "big person" because we learned it from our Dad.

We should be known for being the "big person" because we learned it from our Dad. We should want to be known as the child who looks and acts just like their Dad!

Spend some time in praise and worship of your *Abba*. Then ask Him to pull you up on his lap and hold you in His arms. Ask Him to teach you what it means to be His beloved child. Ask Him to let you see yourself through His eyes. If you struggle in this area, ask a trusted friend to pray for you. God is faithful to answer prayers prayed in His will. His will and desire is for you to be His beloved child, and to know and understand it in your heart and mind.

TRUTHS TO EMBRACE

_____

_____

_____

_____

_____

Week 6

PRAYER: THE KEY

This week we will learn what prayer is and how we can effect reconciliation by the way we pray. Prayer creates unity. When we pray for or with someone, it creates a supernatural bond of unity. Prayer is where those of us who are "fixers" do our best work, because we can take the problem to the only One who can truly fix things. Prayer is not an option. All believers are called to pray.

DAY 1
On Your Knees, All the Time

DAY 2
Postures of Prayer

DAY 3
Praying for Your Irritant

DAY 4
Praying with Your Irritant

DAY 5
But I Didn't Do It!

ON YOUR KNEES, ALL THE TIME

When you pray, go into your room, close the door and pray to your Father, who is unseen. Then your Father, who sees what is done in secret, will reward you.

Matthew 6:6

The only time I watch football is when the University of Texas is playing, since that is the school from which my husband and I both graduated. One Thanksgiving when we were watching the game, I noticed that every time the quarterback left the field, he put on a set of headphones. I wondered why he didn't just walk over and talk to the coach who was standing on the field, so I asked my husband. He told me that throughout the game, the offensive coordinator stays in a box located at the top of the stadium. Since this coach can see the entire field, the quarterback relies on him to call the plays. After he receives his instructions through the headset, the quarterback goes back on the field and calls the plays for the rest of the team. A good quarterback does not call plays based on what he sees or feels – he relies on the coach who can see the "big picture."

We must learn to rely on our heavenly Father who sees the "big picture" from His eternal viewpoint.

In a similar way, we must learn to rely on our heavenly Father who sees the "big picture" from His eternal viewpoint. Prayer is the "headset" that we wear in order to hear the plays called from the heavenly realm. Just like the quarterback, we may experience times when we have to carry out plays that we don't understand – because we are looking at the field only from our vantage point – and we must lay our feelings aside for the God's glory and the good of the team.

Prayer is our means of communication with our Father. There are many aspects of prayer. As believers, we are called to pray without ceasing, to be in constant communication with our holy God. We come in praise, in thanksgiving, in joy, in sorrow, in repentance, with requests, seeking direction, and for numerous other reasons. This week we will focus on how we are to pray as ministers of reconciliation.

I have always had a heart to pray for people and situations, but I have realized that many times I have used prayer as a pious outlet for "Judy, the fixer." I looked at situations through my eyes and heart and just wanted them to get better or be gone.

What I missed was asking God what His plan was. I often overlooked the fact that we sometimes have to go through difficulties for God's refining process to work. Even worse, I took my eyes off of Jesus.

Anytime our focus is off the Lord, our perception is skewed. When our eyes are on the problem, we are praying to patch up the person instead of to glorify God. We must remind ourselves of why we were created. We were created to glorify the Lord and to worship Him. Just like the quarterback relied on his coach, we need to ask for God's perspective. We need to pray with His eyes and His heart, not from the field of our own limited vision and feelings.

Anytime our focus is off the Lord, our perception is skewed.

In Luke 9:29, what happened to Jesus when He was praying? _____
_____
_____

We see here an important lesson about prayer. *Prayer changes us*.

Read 1 Samuel 7:15-8:6 and answer the following questions.

Who was Samuel? _____

Whom did Samuel choose as his successor?_____

How did the people respond?_____

How do you think this made Samuel feel toward his sons and the children of Israel?
_____

Has anyone ever turned their back on you? How did it make you feel? How did you handle the situation? _____
_____
_____
_____

What did Samuel do? _____

The Hebrew word translated *pray* is *palal*. It means to pray, intervene, mediate, or judge.[1] When we are facing difficult situations, it is important that we ask God to show us His perspective, so that we can "judge" the situation correctly. Notice that before Samuel spent time in prayer, he felt as though the people were turning against him, but after prayer, he was able to judge correctly.

In 1 Samuel 8:7, God revealed the reality of the situation to Samuel. Who were the people really turning against? _____

_____

Read Samuel 12.

Even though the people turned against Samuel's leadership, where did Samuel place his focus? What was he compelled to do as a result? _____

_____

_____

How did he change his response to the situation? _____

_____

After praying, Samuel was able to see the people through God's eyes, whereas before praying he was too close to see the situation clearly.

Read Matthew 6:6 below.

> *But you, when you pray, go into your room and when you have*
> *shut your door, pray to your Father who is in the secret place;*
> *and your Father who sees in secret will reward you openly.*
> *(NKJV)*

The Greek word translated *room* is *tameion*, meaning an inner chamber.[2] The Greek word translated *shut* is *kleio*, meaning to shut up compassion or to be devoid of pity toward one.[3]

How does your compassion or pity for people affect your prayer life? _____

_____

_____

I believe the "secret room" is the state of our hearts where our thoughts and will join with our Father's, and we are changed. It is the place where we pray powerfully for others because we are able to judge correctly in intercession. We can see from His vantage point and not through our own compassion, pity, or emotions.

Read 1 Corinthians 2:9-16.

How did God reveal His truth to us? _____

_____

How is it possible for us to see through God's eyes? _____

_____

What kind of person makes judgments? _____

What are God's promises to us in this passage? _____

_____

_____

What does it mean to your prayer life to have the "mind of Christ"? _____

_____

_____

According to Luke 22:39-44, what is the mind of Christ? _____

_____

_____

How do you know this type of abandonment to the Father's will is a lifestyle and not a habit? _____

_____

_____

Write out James 5:16. _____

_____

_____

_____

In the Greek, the word *righteous* is *dikaios*. It means without prejudice or partiality,

I believe the "secret room" is the state of our hearts where our thoughts and will join with our Father's, and we are changed.

A righteous person prays on behalf of another from God's vantage point.

wholly conformed to the will of God.[4] A righteous person prays on behalf of another from God's vantage point. He does not pray with prejudice about a situation; he prays through God's eyes and for His glory. That is why his prayer puts forth so much power.

According to John 14:13-14, what will Jesus do with our requests if we ask "in His name"? _____

_____

What does the phrase, "in My name," mean in the following scriptures? The first one is done for you.

John 14:26 _According to the way the Holy Spirit teaches_ _____

Matthew 18:5 _____

Mark 16:17-18 _____

Luke 21:12-13 _____

Our God is all that we need. He is our Friend, our Deliverer, our Mighty Counselor, the Prince of Peace, God almighty.

Our God is all that we need. He is our Friend, our Deliverer, our Mighty Counselor, the Prince of Peace, God almighty. He has carried us since birth and has promised to take care of us. He is God, and there is none like Him. His plan and purpose will go forward because there is nothing more powerful than our God. It is very important that we understand that God does have a plan for our life and the lives of those around us, that fits into His overall master plan. You and I do not have the foresight to see His big picture. We must trust Him in love and obedience.

Read Matthew 26:53-54. Jesus has the power of heaven at His disposal, but what is most important to Him? _____

_____

_____

Read Hebrews 5:7 and Luke 22:39-44. Does Jesus understand what it is like to pray passionate prayers? _____ What was most important to Him?

_____

Jesus is our example. He was more focused on God than on the situation. To be effective prayer warriors, we need to keep our focus on the Lord, not the circumstances. Circumstances are no big deal for God to orchestrate. If He could part the Red Sea and raise people from the dead, He can change circumstances. God is more concerned with our character.

Jesus is our example. He was more focused on God than on the situation.

Being a very legalistic person by nature, I took the phrase, "ask in Jesus' name," literally for years. I treated it as my credit card. If I wanted God to answer my prayer, I needed to end it by asking my request in Jesus' name. Of course, my legalism was totally off base.

Write out what it means to you to offer prayer to your Father "in the name of Jesus."

_____
_____
_____
_____
_____

In David's prayer in Psalm 141, where does he tell us his eyes are fixed? _____
_____

What does Psalm 139 tell us about being honest with God? _____
_____
_____

You might as well be honest with God because He already knows your innermost thoughts. The good news is that you can ask Him to reveal the wrong thinking in your life. You can ask Him to give you His perspective on a situation. It will totally change your prayer life when you look through His eyes and with His heart.

Read Isaiah 46:3-4 and write God's promise to us in this passage._____
_____
_____
_____

According to Isaiah 46:5-9, should God ever be our Plan B? _____
_____

Name an instance when you thought you had a better plan than God. What was the outcome? _____

_____

What does Isaiah 45:10-11 tell us about God's sovereignty? _____

_____

_____

How does knowing this truth affect your prayer life? _____

_____

_____

We live in a very goal-oriented society. We form mission statements at work, at church, and on committees. We want to know what our goals are and how we can best accomplish them. Our mission statements also tell those on the outside what our central purpose is. As a conclusion to today's study, formulate your own personal mission statement as a prayer warrior in the ministry of reconciliation.

```
┌─────────────────────────────────────────────┐
│           T R U T H S   T O   E M B R A C E  │
│  _____   │
│  _____   │
│  _____   │
│  _____   │
│  _____   │
│  _____   │
└─────────────────────────────────────────────┘
```

POSTURES OF PRAYER

He (Solomon) stood on the platform and then knelt down before the whole assembly of Israel and spread out his hands toward heaven.

2 Chronicles 6:13

Several years ago a boy in our youth group was headed in the wrong direction. Although he had been raised in church with godly parents, he ran around with the wrong crowd and started drinking. One evening, he woke up in the middle of the night to find his mother kneeling at his bedside praying. Startled and confused, he asked her how long she had been there. She replied, "Oh, about three years."

The fact that his mother had been consistently praying for him for three years made such an impact on him that he never drank again.

God is amazing. I'm sure there were some nights that this mother felt discouraged over the fact that she didn't see results as quickly as she had hoped. Yet, she kept her eyes focused on the Lord and not the circumstances. She prayed through God's heart and waited patiently on His timing and plan. The result was not a mere patch on her son's life, but a total life change. I saw that young man turn from his rebellious lifestyle to a life committed to Jesus.

Since that time, I've encouraged many wives and mothers to take time to pray next to their children and husband's bedsides. I have seen God answer these prayers over and over. I believe He honors our humble and heartfelt prayers of obedience when we engage in this posture of prayer through His heart and His eyes. And since we spend a lot of time in bed – it is our place of rest and restoration – what better place to pray for God's sovereignty in the lives of our loved ones?

Read 2 Chronicles 6:13.

In Hebrew the phrase, *knelt down on his knees,* refers to kneeling in worship, based on the fact that God has blessed us and we adore Him.[5]

King Solomon knelt in worship and honor, because of his love and adoration of his heavenly Father.

It was highly unusual for a king to kneel in worship. Normally, the king's subjects would kneel in honor and reverence in his presence. But King Solomon knew that there was Someone else who was the ultimate King and authority, and that was Jehovah-God. King Solomon knelt in worship and honor, because of his love and adoration of his heavenly Father. He did this privately and publicly, thereby teaching Israel how to worship by his actions. Because he knew and understood God's mercies, he had no other choice but to fall on his knees as his reasonable act of worship.

In the New Testament, the words *worship* and *kneel* are used interchangeably depending on the version of the Bible that you are reading. Both words mean to fall upon the knees and touch the ground with the forehead in an expression of profound reverence. It shows homage to someone of superior rank. It is used of an attitude of prayer.

Read the following scriptures and write how and why you know the person is worshipping God.

Matthew 8:2 _____

Matthew 9:18 _____

Matthew 17:14-21 _____

These people knelt in worship. They praised God because they knew that only He possessed the power to heal and restore.

Read Genesis 22:1-14.

What did Abraham and Isaac go up on the mountain to do? _____
_____
_____

What did Abraham do (verse 13)? _____
_____

In order to look up, you must first be looking down. In this instance, Abraham had gone up the mountain to worship the Lord. Scripture tells us that when he looked up, he saw a ram in the thicket. The type of thicket native to this area was a small thorn bush, so that means in order to "look up" to a small bush, Abraham must have had his forehead to the ground.

What do you learn about worship and sacrifice from this passage in Genesis 22?

_____

_____

_____

_____

Read 2 Chronicles 7:1-4.

Why could the priest not enter the temple after Solomon finished praying? _____

_____

_____

_____

What did the Israelites do? Why? _____

_____

_____

When was the sacrifice offered? _____

_____

Which do you think God desires first, sacrifice or worship? Why? _____

_____

_____

_____

Imagine a Sunday morning church service in which the pastor opened in a prayer of worship, honor, and praise of the Lord, and the Lord's glory so filled the sanctuary that we could not continue with business as usual. Suddenly the order of worship, the prayer requests, our tithes and offerings, the planned music would seem of no value and out of place for that time. Our only response, our only desire, our only reasonable act of worship would be to fall on our knees and then our face in praise, worship, and adoration of our holy God. There might be a time later to bring Him our requests, but for that time all we could do would be to focus on Him in love with all our heart, soul, mind, and strength, for He alone is worthy.

This was the experience of the children of Israel when they came to dedicate the temple. This can be a reality for us. Father God desires our worship over our sacrifice. In fact, we are not even capable of offering a suitable sacrifice. That is why He sent Jesus to become the perfect sacrifice for us. We were created to worship the Lord.

Read 2 Chronicles 7:11-22. What did God promise Solomon? _____
_____
_____
_____

Read Luke 22:39-46.

What did Jesus tell the disciples to do? _____
_____
_____

Why do you think He told them twice? _____
_____
_____

What and how did Jesus pray? _____

The disciples were focused   _____

on the problem instead of   _____

the Lord. Any time we are   How did the disciples' prayer time differ from Jesus' prayer time? How did this affect

more focused on the   how they emerged after praying? _____

problem than on the   _____

Father, we are praying in   _____

our own strength.   _____

In verse 45, Scripture tells us that the disciples were asleep, exhausted from sorrow. The word translated *from* in the Greek is used for any kind of separation of one thing from another by which the union or fellowship of the two is destroyed.[6] The disciples were focused on the problem instead of the Lord. Any time we are more focused on the problem than on the Father, we are praying in our own strength. We therefore become exhausted. Instead of attempting to pray our own plans into action, we need to say with Jesus, "Not my will, but Yours."

Unlike the disciples who were exhausted from the separation and trying to pray in their own strength, Jesus was _____ by an angel while praying.

Jesus kept His eyes on His Father.

As a result, He was able to pray more earnestly even though He was in anguish. The Greek word translated *anguish* is *agonia,* meaning a struggle for victory.[7] Jesus kept His eyes on His Father. He was struggling in prayer for spiritual victory so that God's glory would show forth instead of His own agenda. Just as God's glory was revealed through Solomon's prayer, Jesus also prayed for God's glory.

Like Jesus, when we kneel down in an attitude of prayer to place our requests, our circumstances, or our burdens at His feet so that we no longer carry them, we finally come to the place where we give Father God the problems and the solutions. It is the place where we finally "give up" and walk in His strength and not our own. We give up our pride, our agendas, our anger, and our unforgiveness. We focus on God and not the problem so that our wills become one, and we pray with His heart and His mind. God is glorified through our prayer.

We focus on God and not the problem so that our wills become one, and we pray with His heart and His mind.

Fill in the blank from James 5:16: *The prayer of a righteous man is* _____
_____ .

Summarize what you have learned in today's lesson and then spend time in prayer with the Lord.

```
╔══════════════════════════════════════════╗
║          T R U T H S   T O   E M B R A C E          ║
║  _____  ║
║  _____  ║
║  _____  ║
║  _____  ║
║  _____  ║
║  _____  ║
╚══════════════════════════════════════════╝
```

PRAYING FOR YOUR IRRITANT

But I tell you: Love your enemies and pray for those who persecute you, that you may be sons of your Father in heaven.

Matthew 5:44-45

As ministers of reconciliation, we have a higher calling than others.

There have been many times when I have cried out to the Lord asking Him why I was placed in my adoptive family. It always seemed that I didn't fit. There were so many times of heartache and division between my mother and me. Yet, I knew that I was there because of God's sovereignty and not because of an accident.

One day I was sitting in my ladies' Bible study class during a time of testimony following our yearly retreat, when I heard that small, still voice ask, *Did it ever occur to you that I placed you in this family to pray for your mother?* Well, I can honestly say that it had never occurred to me.

At that time, my mother and I were having problems, and I had been praying occasionally, but strictly out of obedience. When I went to God in prayer, at the end I would quietly add, *And I pray for my mother too,* because I knew I should.

After the retreat, I went home and wrote out a prayer for my mother. I could write out the correct words with more objectivity than I could say them. For a while, I just read my prayer to God. Then, I was able to say it without reading it. Eventually, I was able to pray from my heart with God's love.

I can't tell you that it's changed my mother, but it certainly has changed me. Through this time, God softened my heart and gave me His eyes for my mother.

As ministers of reconciliation, we have a higher calling than others. The way we treat each other in the body, how we resolve conflicts, and how we respond to others speak volumes about Christ in us. If we are going to be ministers, then there must be something different about us. Why would anyone want to be a Christian or part of our fellowship if there is not a positive difference of love, grace, and mercy in us?

Read Matthew 5:44-47.

The word translated *love* in this passage is the Greek word *agape* – love that makes the active choice to seek the highest good of another.[8]

With this definition in mind, write out this passage in your own words. _____

_____

_____

_____

_____

We must understand that the fruit of our prayers may never be fully realized by us. We are not praying for our irritant – the person or thing that is bothering us – because it will change them or the situation. We are praying because we are commanded to in God's Word. This prayer will change us and glorify God. It may also change our irritant or our situation; but if it doesn't, know that we serve a God who understands exactly how we feel and the anger, hurt, or frustration that we are experiencing.

We are praying because we are commanded to in His Word.

Read Psalm 55.

This passage was written during a time when King Saul and his men were pursuing David with the intention of killing him. David was the king's son-in-law, comforter, and friend. The two men had once enjoyed a close relationship, but now David was the king's enemy.

Where was David's focus in this prayer? _____

_____

What do you learn about his heart for God, his friend, and his situation? _____

_____

_____

_____

_____

_____

Read 1 Samuel 24.

Would you describe David as a minister of reconciliation? Why? _____

_____

_____

What effect did this have on Saul? _____

_____

_____

Have you ever been betrayed by a friend? How did you handle it? In light of today's lesson, what would you do differently, and how do you think that might affect the outcome? _____

_____

_____

_____

Praying for our irritant means asking God to give us His heart for that person and to teach us through the situation. Praying for our irritant changes us and releases God to work in the life of the other person.

Praying for our irritant means asking God to give us His heart for that person and to teach us through the situation.

Praying for your irritant *is not*:
- praying with an agenda.
- praying to "fix" them.
- praying to be in control.
- praying to get your way.

Praying for your irritant *is*:
- Praying to judge correctly.
- Praying for understanding.
- Praying for God's will – not yours.
- Giving God the problem and the solution.
- Accepting God's timing.
- Extending the full measure of God's love.

God doesn't always answer prayers the way we would like for Him to, but like David, we can trust Him to do what's best.

Read Genesis 20.

Would you consider Abimelech an irritant to Abraham? Why? _____

_____

_____

Do you think that it would have been hard for Abraham to pray for Abimelech? Why? _____

_____

_____

How was Abimelech affected by Abraham's prayer? _____

_____

_____

What do you learn about God from this passage? _____

_____

When God allowed Satan to come against Job, everything dear to Job was destroyed. His friends came to offer words of comfort, but they ultimately accused him of unconfessed sin. Job, however, stood firm in the Lord.

What does Job 32:1-3 tell us Job's friends did? _____

_____

How would you feel toward your friends if, when disaster struck, your friends said it was because of sin in your life? _____

_____

_____

_____

According to Job 42:7-10, how were Job's friends affected after Job prayed for them?

_____

_____

How was Job affected? _____

_____

Read Acts 6:1-10. Write out a description of Stephen. _____

_____

_____

According to Acts 6:8-15, what did Stephen do wrong? _____

_____

_____

After Stephen was brought to trial and he answered the accusations, what did his accusers do (Acts 7:54-60)? _____

_____

_____

_____

What did Stephen do with his dying breath? _____

_____

_____

Only in God's power, strength, and grace could Stephen pray for the very people who were stoning him to death.

Only in God's power, strength, and grace could Stephen pray for the very people who were stoning him to death. Stephen is a powerful example to us of what God can do if we get out of the way and allow Him to work His strength through us. We are not capable of such self-sacrifice on our own. It takes the power of the Father God in us. Stephen prayed with God's heart and will. Stephen wasn't trying to control; he only loved. He accepted that in God's timing he wouldn't see the outcome; it didn't matter because he had given Father God the problem and the solution, and through that he was ushered into the arms of Jesus. And the lives of those he touched were never the same.

We cannot always know the scope of a situation in which God has placed us. One of the men Stephen prayed for was a young Pharisee named Saul who later became the apostle Paul.

When we finally grasp the concept of God's grace, we realize that we are capable of the lowest depth of depravity. We are no better than our irritant, and apart from the Lord, we could actually be that person.

Stephen prayed with God's heart and will. Stephen wasn't trying to control; he only loved.

God's Word says that we are to be perfect as He is perfect, and that we all miss that mark. God is our only measuring stick. Therefore, we can pray with love and acceptance for our irritant because that is how God views us.

Ask God to give you His heart for your irritant. Ask Him to allow you to be His vessel to extend the full extent of His love to that person. Ask Him what He wants you to learn from this situation. Ask Him to teach you grace and give you His power to pray.

TRUTHS TO EMBRACE

_____
_____
_____
_____
_____
_____

Week Six, Day Four

PRAYING
WITH YOUR IRRITANT

Again, I tell you that if two of you on earth agree about anything you ask for, it will be done for you by my Father in heaven.

Matthew 18:19

Today's lesson is more difficult than yesterday's because, like true reconciliation, it requires action. Too often we Christians are more than happy to pray *for* or *about* someone, or even enlist our entire group to do the same, but we are not willing to come honestly before the Lord *with* that person and give God the problem and the solution. What a difference it would make in the church if we resolved our differences with prayer!

It's not always an easy thing to do. Yet, I have never regretted the times that I have laid down my pride and sought the Lord with the person who is bothering me, my "irritant." There have been many times when I have regretted *not* doing that! My heart breaks when I think about the times I lost my temper with a sister in Christ instead of asking her to seek the Lord with me when we were at odds in our relationship.

Read Acts 4:31-34. What happened to the believers when they prayed together?

_____

_____

The outcome of this kind of thinking and focus was that there were no _____ persons among them (verse 34).

How can we be needy when there is division between us? _____

_____

How do you think Proverbs 14:21 fits into praying with your irritant? _____

_____

_____

Write out Matthew 18:19._____

_____

_____

_____

When "two or three agree" about anything and come together in Jesus' name, it does not necessarily mean they agree on the point of their conflict. But they can agree to seek God's will instead of either person's agenda. Agreeing together can be coming to God in humble and honest prayer saying you are at odds over an issue and you are both giving God the problem for His solution. There is tremendous kingdom power in this type of prayer because when you are in God's agreement, you are bound together, unified by the Holy Spirit.

Write out Ecclesiastes 4:9 and 12. _____
_____
_____
_____

When you are in God's agreement, you are bound together, unified by the Holy Spirit.

We can find many seemingly good reasons to justify our feelings and actions when we are wronged or are in conflict with another believer. By the world's standards, we have every right to stand our ground or react in anger, but we are not of this world. Jesus is our standard.

We are not of this world. Jesus is our standard.

Match the following "good reasons" with God's reason.

_____Why should I do all the work?   A. Matthew 5:11
_____I worked for this and deserve it.   B. Mark 7:9
_____But this seems right.   C. Luke 6:29
_____This is the way we've always done it.   D. Matthew 5:7
_____They don't deserve it.   E. Luke 16:15
_____This just doesn't make sense.   F. Matthew 5:10
_____I didn't do anything wrong.   G. John 4:37-38

To whom should you turn when you need direction for solving a conflict?
_____
_____

When we have a conflict that needs to be resolved, Scripture shows us that Jesus is the One to whom we should turn to for direction and resolution.

Read Luke 10:38-40.

What was Martha's viewpoint? _____
What was Mary's viewpoint? _____
What was the Lord's viewpoint? _____
_____

Read Matthew 9:14-17.

What was John's disciples' viewpoint?_____

What was Jesus' disciples' viewpoint?_____

What was the Lord's viewpoint? _____

_____

Read Matthew 15:1-20.

What was the Pharisee's viewpoint?_____

What was the disciples' viewpoint?_____

What was the Lord's viewpoint? _____

_____

Now think of an unresolved conflict you've had with another believer.

What was your viewpoint?_____

What was their viewpoint?_____

God's Word promises us that when we seek Him for direction, He will provide. Seek God in honest and humble prayer and ask Him to show you His viewpoint.

Study the following scriptures, and in your own words, write out God's promise to you.

Jeremiah 29:13 _____

_____

Daniel 2:47_____

_____

Isaiah 48:17_____

_____

Proverbs 18:10 _____

_____

Praying with our irritant takes the focus off of us and puts it on God. Suddenly, both our irritant and the situation look different.

Praying with our irritant takes the focus off of us and puts it on God. Suddenly, both our irritant and the situation look different.

What do each of the following scriptures tell us about trusting God with the outcome of our prayers?

Proverbs 21:30 _____
_____

Proverbs 19:21 _____
_____

Ephesians 2:14 _____
_____

Too often we pray for direction and unity when what we really mean is that we want God to change that person or group over to our way of thinking. Lip service is meaningless since God knows our heart.

Can you look back at times when you prayed together with a brother or sister in Christ, and although your prayer sounded pious, changing them was exactly what you meant to pray for?

Praying with your irritant involves laying down your agenda, laying down your pride, laying down your time schedule, and just saying to the Lord that you have not been in agreement and that you want His perspective, His unity, and His will alone in the situation.

I hope today that you will make a commitment to encourage prayer between you and other believers in the future when there is a problem. You be the one who asks, "Can we give this to the Lord together and seek His direction? Will you pray with me?"

Seek Father God for direction if there is someone in your fellowship with whom you have unresolved issues. It may be that you need to go to them in honesty and openness and ask them to pray with you for God's restoration and

reconciliation. But be certain that you are directed by God, because only His timing is perfect.

Remember, you can only be responsible for your response, not someone else's; however, let your response be one of love through God's heart.

Write out your prayer of commitment to be God's minister of reconciliation through prayer.

TRUTHS TO EMBRACE

_____

_____

_____

_____

_____

_____

BUT I DIDN'T DO IT!

I urge, then first of all, that requests, prayers, intercession and thanksgiving be made for everyone – for kings and all those in authority.

1 Timothy 2:1-2a

Sometimes after our weekly Bible study, several women meet for lunch. We are all from different churches and denominations, so the conversation is always interesting. One day one of the women expressed her concern for discipleship in her church. She was concerned that many of their members fell between the cracks after salvation, or simply became eternal pew sitters, stagnant in their growth. Several other women at the table expressed the same concern. A few offered suggestions on how they thought the problem should be fixed.

Later at home I pondered the situation as I asked the Lord for His view on corporate repentance – the turning of the church as a whole to God. He showed me that the problem is not a lack of discipleship or mentoring programs. The problem is in the hearts of the people, and instead of trying to treat the symptoms, we need to seek God and ask Him to reveal the root of the disease. As a corporate body, we need to seek His face with true repentance in our hearts. The problem is, we love ourselves more than we love God.

As a corporate body, we need to seek His face with true repentance in our hearts. The problem is, we love ourselves more than we love God.

As ministers of reconciliation, you and I must lead by example. We must be the ones who step out first to pray for forgiveness and repentance of sin for our corporate body. Division in the church has pushed many people away from God. Reconciliation through repentance will draw the church and a lost world to Jesus. Whether or not we actually committed each corporate sin is not important. We know that we are capable of anything apart from the grace of God. As a unified body, whatever sin is in our church affects everyone. Through our love for God, we are compelled to pray for the spiritual health of our church as a whole, so the entire church body will come to a place of corporate repentance, seeking God's forgiveness for our lack of love, lack of caring, selfishness, division, zeal for legalism, and desire for manmade doctrine over Christ Jesus and His Word.

Write out 1 Timothy 4:5. _____

_____

_____

_____

When we have become so zealous for our manmade doctrines, not only are we guilty of not loving others, but we are also guilty of not honoring Christ and His Word.

When we have become so zealous for our manmade doctrines, not only are we guilty of not loving others, but we are also guilty of not honoring Christ and His Word. It is then we become like the Pharisee.

Read Luke 18:10-14.

How did the Pharisee view himself? _____

_____

_____

Has there ever been a time when you have prayed for your church but your heart attitude was that of a Pharisee? _____

What was the heart attitude of the tax collector? How would his grasp of grace have affected your prayer? _____

_____

_____

_____

A few years ago, there was a group of people who followed the course taken by the Christians during the "Crusades." Throughout their journey, on behalf of their ancestors, they asked forgiveness from the descendants of the people who were attacked "in the name of Jesus." As a result, wounds that had festered for hundreds of years were healed.

Read Hosea 7:13-16.

What was the heart attitude of the people? Was there repentance?_____

_____

_____

_____

What did God long to do? _____

Read Hosea 8:2-6.

What hindered God from carrying out His plans? _____
_____

For what pupose had the people gathered together? _____
_____

Read Joel 2:12-19.

What does God desire? _____
_____

What do you think the difference is between Joel 2:19 and Hosea 7:14?_____
_____
_____

Throughout the Scriptures, we read of oil being used to consecrate something for a sacred use. Oil was used for healing, and it also symbolized the Holy Spirit. I believe that the grain in these verses symbolizes our needs for which God provides, the new wine symbolizes our salvation through the blood of Jesus, and the oil symbolizes the repentant heart healed and restored by the Holy Spirit.

God promised that if His people would give Him their hearts, their sin, then He would send them grain, new wine, and oil, and only this would satisfy them.

In Hosea, Jehovah longed to redeem His children, but their hearts were evil and unrepentant. They cried out for what they wanted, but their hearts did not seek forgiveness of sin. The phrase, *gathered together for grain and new wine,* means that they cried out to God for what they needed or wanted, and to be His child, but they wouldn't confess their sin. They showed no genuine repentance. In Joel, God promised that if His people would give Him their hearts, their sin, then He would send them grain, new wine, and oil, and only this would satisfy them.

Beloved, we search for all kinds of things to satisfy us. We think that if others would just get their acts together at church, then we would see a great movement of God. Based on the fact that we are His children, we come together for prayer meetings with pages of "grain" – prayer requests, desires, things that we want God to fix. But God isn't a catalog from which to order.

He is our holy, righteous God who desires our hearts. He sent His only Son to die for our sins. He wants us to confess that sin and get our hearts right before Him.

What a difference we would see if at prayer meetings, we came before God and confessed corporate sin with genuine repentance. If we will, His Word promises us that He will then take care of our needs.

God isn't a catalog from which to order. He is our holy, righteous God who desires our hearts.

Fill in the blanks from Joel 2:19.

I am sending _____, _____, and _____ enough to satisfy you fully.

Does God hear our prayers? Is He affected by them? Can one man's plea change the fate of a nation?

Read Exodus 33 and write your answer. _____
_____

Read 1 Samuel 2:22-36. Describe Eli and his sons._____
_____

According to 1 Samuel 1:21-28, where was Samuel raised?_____
_____

What did the Lord teach Samuel about individual and corporate repentance (1 Samuel 3:1-21)? _____
_____
_____
_____

Read 1 Samuel 7:2-6.

In verse 5, the word translated *intercede* is the Hebrew word *palal*, meaning to pray, to intervene, to mediate, or to judge.[9]

What did Samuel lead the Israelites to do? _____
_____

What did he agree to do? _____

Why do you think he had such a passion for repentance? _____
_____
_____

Samuel saw firsthand the devastation experienced by Eli, his sons, and their families because of sin. Eli chose not to repent of his own sin, and as a result, his entire family was affected. Samuel learned this lesson as a young boy, and he carried the precept throughout his ministry.

We need to be as astute as Samuel. Individual and corporate sin affects the entire church body, and we are each held accountable for the attitudes of our hearts. We are also called to intercede for the body of Christ. This includes standing in the gap for confession of sin.

Individual and corporate sin affects the entire church body, and we are each held accountable for the attitudes of our hearts.

Read Nehemiah 1:4-11.

What does Nehemiah pray? _____
_____

In 1 Timothy 2:1, what does God's Word command us to do? Why? _____
_____
_____

In Ephesians 3:14-19, what did Paul pray? _____
_____

In Philippians 1:9-11? _____
_____
_____

In Colossians 1:9-14? _____
_____

How would that bring about repentance? _____
_____
_____

Write out God's promise to you from Joshua 23:10. _____

_____

What does that mean to you and your prayer life? _____

_____

In His Word, God has commanded us to pray for the body of Christ. We are commanded to confess our sins, and He will cleanse us from unrighteousness. As ministers of reconciliation, we are to lead by example. You can make a difference in the lives of those for whom you pray. We know that because Father God gave us His promise, and He is always true.

As ministers of reconciliation, we are to lead by example.

I challenge you today and from now on to be on your knees for your church, your neighborhood, your city, and your nation. Pray that we will have softened hearts turned to God. Confess your sin, and confess our corporate sin. We are affected by the sins of our fathers and our church, past and present, whether we personally committed them or not. Today, confess them. Break the chains, and let God bring you and your fellowship the grain, new wine, and oil, enough to satisfy you fully.

TRUTHS TO EMBRACE

_____

_____

_____

_____

_____

_____

Week 7

RELATIONSHIPS

Too often in life we are ruled by our feelings. We are hurt or disappointed in our relationships because the other person involved does not meet our expectations. Or we may go through life always expecting others to hurt us or let us down. Either way, our focus is wrong. My friend always says that we should trust God and love people. Only Father God is worthy of our complete and total trust. This week we will explore different relationships, and our feelings, expectations, and eternal back-up plan. I pray that as we enter this week of study, you will ask your *Abba* Father to make you open to see the truth about yourself and your relationships.

DAY 1
Unrealistic Expectations

DAY 2
Jesus in Me

DAY 3
Friends

DAY 4
The Body of Christ

DAY 5
Altars

Week Seven, Day One

UNREALISTIC EXPECTATIONS

To Him who is able to do immeasurably more than all we ask or imagine, according to his power that is at work within us.

Ephesians 3:20

In her book, *Managing Your Emotions*, Joyce Meyer writes that we should not look to other people to meet our needs, but rather look to the Lord to fulfill our needs as He knows what is best for us.[1]

> *Unrealistic expectations are the opposite of God's grace because grace doesn't expect anything.*

Every time we look to someone other than God to meet our needs, including ourselves, we put our expectations in the wrong place. We are depending on them. Therefore, the way they respond to our expectations determines how we will feel toward them.

The bottom line becomes this: Our feelings are based on the response of others.

As believers we are commanded not to be led by our feelings. We are commanded to be led by the Spirit. There is no middle ground; as a result, we must make a choice. Will we live our lives placing our expectations on others, and as a result, be continually disappointed? Or will we live our lives embracing God's grace and extending it to others?

Unrealistic expectations are the opposite of God's grace because *grace doesn't expect anything*. Grace is receiving what we don't deserve; expecting is having to meet an agenda or standard. Webster's defines *expectation* as "a looking forward to, anticipation, the probability of the occurrence of something."[2]

If someone doesn't meet your expectations (what you anticipate or desire from them), do they owe you something because you are disappointed and your feelings are hurt? Why? Back up your answer with Scripture. _____

_____

Read James 4:1, substituting the phrase, *unrealistic expectations,* for *desires.* What causes fights and quarrels? _____

_____

According to Colossians 3:13-14 and Ephesians 4:1-3, what are we to do with our unrealistic expectations and feelings toward others when they hurt us or make us angry or frustrated? Why? _____

_____

_____

_____

The word *love* in this passage is translated from the Greek word, *agape*, which we learned earlier means "to actively seek the highest good of another."[3] To love with agape love means choosing not to focus on our own needs and wants and choosing to seek the highest good for another.

If we follow God's precept in these passages, what is the fruit?_____

_____

_____

To love with agape love means choosing not to focus on our own needs and wants and choosing to seek the highest good for another.

Read 2 Timothy 4:14-18. Do you think Paul viewed these people with unrealistic expectations or with grace? Why? _____

_____

_____

Recount a time and the outcome when you had unrealistic expectations for someone. _____

_____

_____

_____

Recount a time and the outcome when you extended grace to someone in a difficult situation. _____

_____

_____

_____

_____

One of the hardest things in preparing for this study was facing my own depravity. Not my depravity prior to salvation, but the deceitful, sinful, depraved person I still am even after walking closely with the Lord for a long time. I had to face the depth of my fleshly nature. Somehow I had thought my life would be cleaned up after having been a Christian for many years; but the reality is that the closer I get to the

Lord, the brighter His light shines deep into the cracks and crevices of my life. Granted, the bigger and more obvious sins are gone, but now the inward thoughts of my heart seem worse than ever.

I'm reminded of when I had lunch with a friend whom I had not seen for several years. As we spent time catching up on our lives, I mentioned that I was writing a Bible study. Her first response was, "I didn't know that you were a writer!" It still makes me smile. I replied, "I'm not. Do you think Father God looked around and asked, 'Who has her act together, is spiritual and knowledgeable, and is a great writer?' No, He said, 'Who do we have that would make it very evident that it is the Holy Spirit writing through her and not her own abilities, talents, and accomplishments? Of course! Let's use Judy Baker!'"

According to Psalm 15, who is worthy? _____

What does Jeremiah 17:9 say about the heart?_____
_____

According to Romans 9:16, on what do we depend or not depend?_____
_____

According to Isaiah 64:6, how worthy are our righteous acts? _____
_____

I don't know about you, but I think of the apostle Paul as someone who did a pretty good job of totally abandoning his life to the Lord and living righteously. Yet in Romans 7:7-8:25, he paints a different picture.

What was Paul's struggle? How did he resolve to live? _____
_____
_____
_____
_____

According to Romans 3:22-24, do we ever get our act together? What is our only hope? _____

Read Genesis 20. Does Abraham meet your expectation for righteousness? Why?
_____
_____

Now read about Abraham in Hebrew 11:8-19 and Romans 4:1-3. Does this sound like the same man? Why? _____

_____

_____

I love the "faith chapter" of Hebrews because *that is our reality in Christ Jesus.* God never whitewashes the truth. In the Old Testament, He pulled no punches about Abraham's sin. I would suppose that there were many times when Abraham did not even meet his own expectations for his life. He was a man called of God, who heard directly from God, and yet he still took matters into his own hands, lied, and sent his wife into the arms of another man, instead of trusting God. Yet, in the New Testament, we see how God saw Abraham – through His eyes of grace. Beloved, He sees you in the same way! He doesn't have unrealistic expectations of you; He simply sees you through grace. All we need to do is accept that grace and appropriate it into our own lives.

In the New Testament, we see how God saw Abraham – through His eyes of grace. He sees you in the same way!

In 1 Corinthians 15:10, the phrase *was not without effect* means *to have spiritual wealth.*

With that in mind, read the verse and write it in your own words. _____

_____

_____

_____

Read Hebrews 4:15-16. What do you think Jesus would say to you when you are struggling with your own depravity and the unrealistic expectations you have of yourself? _____

_____

_____

_____

Trust God and love people. I have dealt with unrealistic expectations for most of my life. I used to set very high standards for myself and for others. The end result was turmoil within me when I met with failure. However, what amazed me about the Father was that He not only consistently met my expectations, He surpassed them. *Father God is our obtainable expectation!*

Look up Isaiah 64:3 and fill in the blanks.

When you did _____ things that we did not _____, you came down, and the mountains trembled before you.

Write out Ephesians 3:20. _____

_____

_____

_____

Look up the following scriptures and write out God's promise that you can always count on.

Isaiah 41:9 _____

Psalm 9:9 _____

Isaiah 26:3 _____

Hebrews 13:5 _____

1 Peter 5:6-10 _____

2 Peter 1:3 _____

Exodus 14:14 _____

Romans 8:38-39 _____

Philippians 4:19 _____

1 John 3:1-2 _____

1 John 3:20 _____

Philippians 1:6 _____

Genesis 15:1 _____

Psalm 4:3 _____

Read Psalm 33 and ponder the God whom you serve. Write out your own psalm of praise to the Father who is your obtainable Expectation.

TRUTHS TO EMBRACE

_____

_____

_____

_____

_____

_____

Week Seven, Day Two

JESUS IN ME

Our clothes say a lot about us.

Since, then, you have been raised with Christ, set your hearts on things above, where Christ is seated at the right hand of God.

Colossians 3:1

A few years ago, I was asked to be in charge of our band booster club's chili supper fundraiser. As the time neared, I continued to put off the planning necessary for such an event. Finally, I was faced with a nearing deadline. In my panic, I thought, *I can do this. Besides, it's not like there's anything spiritual about a chili supper. I've done these before at my child's old school. I just need to get started and put my plan into action.*

Almost immediately, I could feel the gentle hands of my Father on my face, turning my focus toward Him. *Excuse me,* I could almost hear Him say, *but when did you start separating your life at church and school?* Boy, was I busted! After a time of repentance, I prayed, gave Him this chili supper for His glory, and asked what He wanted me to do. Amazingly, God opened several doors for ministry during that time, and the chili supper went off without a hitch. I realized that having Jesus in me is not a part-time relationship, because He desires to live His life through me full time.

What does Galatians 3:1-5 say about having a part-time relationship with Jesus?

_____

_____

Our clothes say a lot about us. Very often, our clothing tells of our values, our priorities, and our interests. Each of my four children has their own style of dressing. This is most evident in my three sons. Not one of them wears the same type or brand of clothing; therefore, they look completely different. However, their clothing choices do tell others a lot about them, their personalities, and where they are in their lives.

Read Galatians 3:26-29 and Isaiah 61:10. In what are we to clothe ourselves? What does that clothing say about us? _____

_____

_____

In her book, *Managing Your Emotions,* Joyce Meyer writes, "You and I need to clothe ourselves with Jesus, to take on His character and personality. We need to quit being so concerned about what others are doing to *us* and become more concerned with what they are doing to *themselves* by the way they are treating us."[4]

In what things are we clothing ourselves when we are more concerned with our own treatment than the treatment of others and the Lord? _____

_____

_____

What is the result of that kind of thinking? _____

_____

_____

Have you ever noticed that when two people spend a lot of time together, they begin to think and speak alike?

Have you ever noticed that when two people spend a lot of time together, they begin to think and speak alike? Many times, they even start to look similar. My best friend and I talk every day. In fact, we usually talk several times a day. Many times when one of us is out alone, we will be asked where the other one is because people are so used to seeing us together. And we normally know exactly where the other one is, as well as knowing her schedule.

Many times, one of us just needs to talk about something out loud, while the other patiently listens. Sometimes one of us just needs a safe place to vent anger, hurt, or frustration. Sometimes we counsel each other on problems. But most of the time, we just share what is going on in our lives.

We rejoice with each other in the good times and cry together in the bad. I know that I can talk to her about anything, and she will still be my friend. There are no rules or barriers of how, when, or what we can say. We have screamed and argued with each other, but we always talk things out until we resolve the issue, because our relationship is not conditional.

After one of us has been out of town, we have to update each other on what has happened while we were apart. I've never liked these times because they don't seem normal for us. We're used to knowing daily what the other is doing. Instead, we have to spend time catching up instead of going forward with our day-to-day friendship.

We are very close because we have chosen to make time for each other. We share our dreams, our hurts, our joys, and our concerns. We understand each other, think alike, and often know each other's thoughts because we are so close.

However, our friendship pales in comparison to what it means to me to be "in Christ Jesus" and have everyone associate me with the Lord. I can't imagine going any-

Nothing can compare to my relationship with Jesus Christ. I share everything with Him, and He knows and understands me in ways that no one else will ever know.

where that I was not clothed in Jesus. Separation from my relationship with Jesus would be evident to all who saw me. He is my first thought in the morning and during the day, and He is my last thought at night. Nothing can compare to my relationship with Jesus Christ. I share everything with Him, and He knows and understands me in ways that no one else will ever know. He is my true safe haven because He has no human limitations. He is never too busy to talk to me or to listen, and He is always available. He is my source, my center, my heart, and my soul.

The thought of having to spend time catching up with Jesus breaks my heart because any time spent apart would mean that I was the one who had neglected the relationship. I tell Him all the time that I want to walk so closely to Him that I step on His feet!

What we should desire most in our lives is that when people look at us, they would see Christ Jesus, because He is what we are to be clothed in from head to toe.

You cannot look at my two oldest sons and not know they are brothers. They look very much alike. They have the same build and many of the same mannerisms. They are just like their dad.

Often when my friend and I are out together, someone asks us if we are sisters. We always enjoy a laugh later because on the outside we look nothing alike! In fact, we have very little in common. But what we do share is a deep abiding commitment and love for the Lord Jesus Christ, a love that covers all of our life. So although we are not biological sisters, we are spiritual sisters. We are sisters in Christ Jesus. What people see is that we both look like our Father.

Our relationship with Christ is why we were created.

According to Mark 3:35, whom does Jesus say is His family? _____

_____

_____

We have an incredibly special, intimate relationship with Father God because of our being "in Christ Jesus." Our relationship with Christ is why we were created. It gives us a reason to get up in the morning because it is our basis for everything, including the way we relate in all of our relationships. It changes the way we view others and ourselves. It changes the way we think, act, and speak. It is our identity and our heritage.

The word *in* in the Greek is *enorkizo*. It denotes a position of rest. It means *in, by,* or *with*. Our position as believers is to walk "in Christ." So our relationship in Christ is one in which we rest in Him and He does the work through us.

At least thirty-four blessings are listed in the New Testament for those who share the relationship "in Christ."

Read the book of Ephesians and list some of the blessings and promises we have through our relationship in Christ.

In Christ, I _____.

In Christ, I _____.

In Christ, I _____.

In Christ, I _____.

In Christ, I _____.

In Christ, I _____.

In Christ, I _____.

In Christ, I _____.

In Christ, I _____.

Our relationship in Christ is one in which we rest in Him and He does the work through us.

In addition, look up the following verses.

2 Corinthians 5:17
In Christ, I _____.

Galatians 3:26
In Christ, I _____.

Philippians 4:7
In Christ, I _____.

Philippians 4:19
In Christ, I _____.

Colossians 2:10
In Christ, I _____.

Romans 8:1
In Christ, I _____.

Without Jesus' living His life through me, I cannot be a woman of grace, forgiveness, tolerance, patience, or unconditional love.

Without Jesus' living His life through me, I cannot be a woman of grace, forgiveness, tolerance, patience, or unconditional love.

Describe who you are "in Christ." How does this change your life, your approach, and your relationships with others? With Jesus? On what promises can you stand? What possibilities are open to you? Write your answer as a prayer of praise to your heavenly Daddy.

TRUTHS TO EMBRACE

_____
_____
_____
_____
_____
_____

FRIENDS

Greater love has no one than this, that he lay down his life for his friends.

John 15:13

One summer, my daughter and a friend planned to go to a sports camp at the University of Texas. However, after we sent in my daughter's registration, her roommate backed out on her. Beth wanted to cancel because she didn't want to go alone, but it was too late for us to get our refund. I explained to her the importance of commitment, and I assured her that she would make new friends at camp. A good friend even told Beth that she went to camp alone every year and always met her new "best friend" that week.

Isn't that typical of women? Give us a week (or even a few hours or days) with a new acquaintance, and we can become what seems like close friends. Yet, we need to remember that a really close friendship takes years to develop and grow. Often the relationship problems that we experience occur precisely because we are expecting an unreasonable level of love and commitment from a casual friend.

Yet, we need to remember that a really close friendship takes years to develop and grow.

According to Proverbs 17:17, what are the limits of a friend's love? _____
_____
_____

What does John 15:13 mean to you? _____
_____

Love is saying, "I want what is best for you."[6] This is agape love, actively seeking the highest good of another based on a decision of your will.

In their book, *Who Will I Be for the Rest of My Life?*, Ruth Vaughn and Anita Higman write that love is saying, "I want what is best for you."[6] This is agape love, actively seeking the highest good of another based on a decision of your will. I must admit that for most of my life I have loved my friends with more of an emotional love followed by a disappointment that they did not love me with a true agape love. I was afflicted with the "what about me" syndrome. I don't think that I am alone in this, because we are by nature a selfish, self-centered people. We look at most situations from the viewpoint of how our relationships affect us.

Write out Proverbs 18:24 in your own words. _____
_____

Jesus had many friends. Twelve of them were close friends, but one of the twelve betrayed him. Of those twelve close friends, there were three to whom He was closest and one was referred to in Scripture as "the one Jesus loved."

Jesus had many friends.

How did Jesus refer to Judas (Matt. 26:47-50)? _____

How did John describe himself (John 13:23)?_____

Read Matthew 26:36-46 and Mark 14:32-34.

Of those twelve close friends, there were three to whom He was closest and one was referred to in Scripture as "the one Jesus loved."

Whom did Jesus take with Him to the Garden of Gethsemane where He would face perhaps His most crucial moment? _____
_____

What did Jesus ask of them?_____

Were these three closest friends a source of support for Jesus? To whose needs were they attending? _____
_____

Have you ever been in a traumatic situation or time of great need, and asked for support from your friends, but they were too tired or too busy to help you? What did you think or feel? What effect did this have on you and your relationship with them? Why? _____
_____
_____
_____

Read Matthew 26:17-35. What did Jesus say His friends would do? What was their response? _____
_____
_____
_____

We have looked at some of these scriptures before, but let's look again for another facet of truth.

According to John 18:15-27, who followed Jesus when He was arrested?
_____
_____

Where do you think the other friends/disciples were? _____
_____
_____

That night after Jesus was arrested, what do you imagine the disciples might have been thinking and feeling? _____
_____

What do you think Peter, James, and John, who were in the inner circle and closest to Jesus, were thinking? Remember, He had asked them to stand by Him in Gethsemane while He prayed and struggled. _____
_____
_____
_____

What might Peter and John have been thinking and feeling while watching Jesus on trial? _____
_____
_____
_____

We are quick to criticize Peter for denying His relationship with Christ, but maybe we need to focus on the fact that of the twelve disciples, Peter was one of only two who even followed Jesus and went to His trial. Perhaps John, being closest to Jesus, was so distraught at falling asleep when Jesus needed him that he suddenly had the courage to stand by Him no matter what the cost. Because of the love Jesus had shown John, John now understood that true love meant actively seeking Jesus' highest good and not his own. What about James? He never even stepped out at all.

It is hard when a friend quietly stands by and watches your being tried and convicted while saying nothing to support you.

When this happens, where is your focus? _____
_____
_____
_____

Is it on "poor me," or are you considering how your suffering might be affecting them? I think when Jesus looked at Peter and John, He saw the strength, love, and horror in their eyes as they helplessly stood by and watched Him be beaten and then crucified.

Have you ever had a situation in which you needed a friend's support and felt that that friend denied you? Explain._____

_____

_____

Looking back, were you a loving friend desiring the best for that person, or were you wanting someone to suffer with you?_____

_____

_____

When my oldest son was five, a boy in my baby-sitting co-op broke his arm in my backyard. At the time, I was pregnant without health insurance, and Bruce was out of work from the oil field crash of the early 1980's. We had already made three claims on our home insurance that year due to a hurricane, frozen water pipes that leaked on Christmas day, and a tornado that had ripped off the roof of our house. The boy's parents both worked and had great insurance benefits, but still they asked us to file a claim on our homeowner's insurance. When I called our insurance agent, he said that they would pay the claim, but that we risked our insurance being cancelled after filing so many claims in one year.

I told the boy's parents and said that I would not stop them from filing, but that I would prefer to not file myself under the circumstances. They replied that if I did not file, they would sue us.

I was very upset, but the most hurtful part was that my other friends continued to baby-sit for this family. I took it as a personal insult. How could they not support me? At the time, I was looking at the situation only from the standpoint of how it affected me, instead of the awkward situation my friends were facing.

Jesus forgave the disciples and even went to them in love to reconcile their relationship. What keeps us from doing that?_____

_____

In his book, *Connecting*, Larry Crabb wrote that there is something within us designed to touch that other soul.[7] Because of the deep, abiding love and connection between Jesus and His disciples, in addition to their feeling guilty for denying Him, they were probably extremely miserable and hurt by what they saw happening to Jesus. So often we focus on our own hurt and pain with no thought of the effect it has on our friends.

Read John 15:12-17. What did Jesus command us to do? _____

_____

There is something within us designed to touch that other soul.

We focus on our own hurt and pain with no thought of the effect it has on our friends.

What does it mean for you to lay down your life for your friend? Does it mean to literally, physically die for them? Does it mean to die to self-interest? Does it mean both? What does it mean in Galatians 2:20? _____

_____

_____

_____

We are to confess our love for Jesus in our words and actions.

I've learned that when I feel bad I become an easy target for Satan's attack. I normally love to do things for people to make them feel special. However, as a woman in my forties with raging hormones, I went through a pity party because I felt like no one reciprocated my acts of kindness. I pouted about this for a while and then I decided to voice my complaint to a friend. After sharing my feelings with her, however, I wished I had never said anything. Since I had previously tried to make her feel special, I was now forced to ask myself when I had lost my focus and started thinking about myself first.

The Bible teaches that we are to confess our love for Jesus in our words and actions. This begins with those closest to us. Scripture commands us to reconcile our relationships.

What does Matthew 5:23-24 teach us?_____

_____

According to John 13:15-17, who is our example?_____

_____

Jesus did not get mad at Peter, James, and John and turn from them because they let Him down.

Notice that Jesus did not get mad at Peter, James, and John and turn from them because they let Him down. Instead, He focused on the hurt and pain that they were experiencing because of their actions.

When someone hurts you, do you ask the Father God for His perspective on the situation? Do you ask to understand the pain in the situation? Do you pray with God's heart for their life?

Agape love and true friendship occur when you put the other person's needs, desires, and hurts above your own.

Agape love and true friendship occur when you put the other person's needs, desires, and hurts above your own. It should no longer be about what others can do for you, but how you can lay down your life for them. Jesus went back as many times as it took to reconcile Peter and the other disciples. Had Jesus done anything wrong? *No!* But His heart broke for His friends who were hurting after abandoning Him in His hour of need.

Write out how Jesus reached out to Peter repeatedly.

Luke 22:61 _____

Mark 16:6-7 _____

John 20:19-23 _____

John 21:1-21 _____

Grace is unlimited; so is

agape love.

Are you willing to go the distance to love your friends and lay down your life for them, or do you give up too easily by just doing the minimum, "legal" requirement? Grace is unlimited; so is agape love.

Look back at John 20:19-23.

What was the first thing Jesus said to His disciples? _____
_____
_____

There is no peace in

division or unforgiveness.

There is no peace in division or unforgiveness.

What did Jesus address as soon as He breathed the Holy Spirit on them? Why?
_____
_____

On our own, we are not capable of following our Lord's command to forgive. We can't forgive friends on our own. The wounds are too deep, too personal, and too intimate, but through the power of the Holy Spirit within us, we can and must!

Think about the people in your life. Who are your close friends? Who are just acquaintances? Who makes up in your inner circle? Of those, who is the one you truly love? I would suggest going to the Lord in prayer with your closest friend and consecrating your friendship to Him for His glory and His use. (See 1 Samuel 20:42.) Pray that you might be a vessel for the Father God to extend His love to your friend. Is there a friend whom you need to forgive? It is time to give that person the free gift of grace that Jesus gave you. Grace demonstrates a love that is not earned or unearned, but is a gift from the Lord God almighty.

TRUTHS TO EMBRACE

_____

_____

_____

_____

_____

_____

THE BODY OF CHRIST

Why do you look at the speck of sawdust in your brother's eye and pay no attention to the plank in your own eye?

Matthew 7:3

Because we were obedient to the Lord and extended His love and grace to one of His needy children, Jesus was able to shine His light into her heart and convict her Himself.

Not long ago, I was in New Orleans to take a seminary class on women's ministry. One night, a group of the ladies in my class decided to go down to the French Quarter to shop and have dinner. One woman and I were walking behind the group when we noticed a very pretty teenage girl who was sitting on the curb holding a sign that said, "Pregnant and Hungry." The woman and I looked at each other and walked on so as not to lose our group; but I just could not leave this girl. I suggested to the other woman that we invite this girl to eat with us, and she agreed. The girl, Lily, accepted our offer and went to tell her boyfriend that she would be back later.

As we walked with Lily to the nearest restaurant, I noticed a sticker on the front of her dirty overalls that said, "I love *sex*!" In the restaurant, we made casual conversation. We asked her how she was feeling and offered suggestions on agencies that could help her with food and medical care. The only mention of God was in the prayer before we ate.

Our standard should be God's perfection, not just being a better Christian.

We told Lily that we were all in school together, but we gave no further details. Not long into the meal, I noticed that Lily had very discreetly removed the sticker and wrapped it around her finger. After we finished eating, we asked her if she knew Jesus, and she assured us that she did. We asked if we could pray with her, and she said that would be fine. We walked outside the restaurant, gathered around her on the sidewalk of the French Quarter, prayed for her, and then said our goodbyes.

The next morning, one of the ladies in our group told me that she had desperately wanted to tell this girl to take off her inappropriate sticker, but that she had not been able to get a word into our conversation. The wonderful thing was that she didn't have to!

Because we were obedient to the Lord and extended His love and grace to one of His needy children, Jesus was able to shine His light into her heart and convict her Himself.

How would you apply 1 Corinthians 2:4 to this situation? _____

_____

_____

The amazing (or should I say "humbling") thing about grace is that when the Father God looked down on that dinner table, He saw no difference between Lily and the rest of us. Our standard should be God's perfection, not just being a better Christian.

In view of God's grace, apply James 2:1-13 to your own walk. _____

_____

_____

According to Philippians 2:5, what is your attitude to be? _____

_____

According to 1 Peter 3:1-5, if someone does not believe the Word of God, how are we to "win" that person over? _____

_____

_____

Does God realize that this can be very costly to us? Explain. _____

_____

_____

_____

Very often, walking the road where we must be quiet and let our life shine before men can be very hard. It takes patience and faith because we usually do not see quick results.

What does the Lord promise us in 1 Corinthians 15:58? _____

_____

_____

_____

How does 1 John 3:18 describe this kind of love? _____

_____

_____

_____

According to Ephesians 5:2, what does Father God consider this life of love?

_____

_____

In 1 Chronicles 22:19, what does God command of us? _____

_____

_____

Don't pick on people, jump

on their failures, and

criticize their faults —

unless, of course, you want

the same treatment.

What a difference it will make in our relationships in the body of Christ when we begin to focus on refining our own walk with the Lord instead of trying to fix our neighbors! I like the way the Message Bible interprets Matthew 7:1-5:

> *Don't pick on people, jump on their failures, and criticize their faults—unless, of course, you want the same treatment. That critical spirit has a way of boomeranging. It's easy to see a smudge on your neighbor's face and be oblivious to the ugly sneer on your own. Do you have the nerve to say, "let me wash your face for you," when your own face is distorted by contempt? It's this whole traveling road show mentality all over again, playing a holier-than-thou part instead of just living your part. Wipe that ugly sneer off your own face, and you might be fit to offer a washcloth to your neighbor.*

Psalm 119 was written by Asaph. Verses 25-27 and 67-71 tell us God in His sovereignty allowed Asaph to go through some trials. What was the value of that?

_____

_____

According to verse 102, who was his teacher? _____

_____

According to Psalm 125:3, does God need our help or guidance? _____

_____

_____

What is the promise on which we can stand when we see a brother or sister living outside of the will of God (2 Samuel 14:14)? _____

_____

_____

Do we need to devise a plan to fix them? Why? _____

_____

Many times God almighty allows trials or problems in our lives in order to refine us. Unless He specifically calls you to step in and offer His wisdom or correction in someone's life, you are probably called to *intercede* in prayer instead of interfere in His plan. God is quite capable of teaching and convicting someone without our help.

I have found that unless He guides me to specifically do so, I am much more effective talking to God about the sin I see in someone else's life than I am talking to them. Otherwise, when I meddle in my self-righteousness, it causes division in the body of Christ.

The Bible tells us that there are times when we are to confront another believer. However, *these are always Holy Spirit led and directed.* All too often, we either choose to gossip among ourselves about the problem, or we just hold on to unforgiveness and bitterness.

How does Matthew 18:15-17 say we are to handle the situation when a brother or sister sins against us? _____
_____
_____
_____

If a church member refuses to repent after you have done all these measures, what are you commanded to do? _____
_____
_____
_____
_____

Read Matthew 9:10-13. How did Jesus treat unbelieving pagans and tax collectors?
_____
_____
_____

Read Luke 22:4-6 and Matthew 26:14-15. What did Judas agree to do? What did he desire more than following Jesus? _____
_____
_____
_____

You are probably called to intercede in prayer instead of interfere in His plan. God is quite capable of teaching and convicting someone without our help.

I am much more effective talking to God about the sin I see in someone else's life than I am talking to them.

Jesus Christ took our sins and died on the cross in our place. In return, He gave us eternal life, His righteousness, and oneness with our heavenly Father by His grace. He then asked us to love one another as He loves us, to forgive one another as He forgives us, and extend the grace that we have received.

Jesus Christ took on our sins and died on the cross in our place.

> *Therefore, as God's chosen people, holy and dearly loved, clothe yourselves with compassion, kindness, humility, gentleness and patience. Bear with each other and forgive whatever grievances you may have against one another. Forgive as the Lord forgave you. And over all these virtues put on love, which binds them all together in perfect unity.*
> *Let the peace of Christ rule in your hearts, since as members of one body you were called to peace. And be thankful. Let the word of Christ dwell in you richly as you teach and admonish one another with all wisdom, and as you sing psalms, hymns and spiritual songs with gratitude in your hearts to God. And whatever you do, whether in word or deed, do it all in the name of the Lord Jesus, giving thanks to God the Father through him.*
>
> *Colossians 3:12-1*

When we refuse to forgive; gossip about people or problems; insist on having our way; create disunity in the body of Christ; let our pride keep us from going to someone with whom we have a problem; or are legalistic in our criticism or judgment of believers, are we any different than Judas?

What is more valuable to you than following Jesus? What is more valuable to you than answering His call for reconciliation in the body of Christ? How long shall we betray Jesus in secret but on Sunday morning put on our public mask? You see, except for the grace of God, we are no different than Judas.

Ask God to give you His love for the body of Christ and praise Him that we are saved and sanctified by His grace and not our works or behavior.

TRUTHS TO EMBRACE

_____

_____

_____

_____

_____

_____

ALTARS

The LORD appeared to Abram and said, "To your offspring I will give this land." So he built an altar there to the LORD, who had appeared to him.

Genesis 12:7

Our most important relationship in life is with our God. Father God is with us at all times, even when we are unaware of Him. However, there are those "mountaintop" experiences when we feel His presence in a mighty way. They are the times when we reach our depths and reach out for Jehovah, and He touches us in a way that totally changes our life. Perhaps you've had a need that has been taken care of by *Jehovah Jireh*, the Lord our Provider. Maybe you've received peace in your circumstances from *Jehovah Shalom*, the Lord our Peace. Maybe you've been given guidance from *Jehovah Rohi*, the Lord our Shepherd, or you were delivered of a stronghold in your life by *Jehovah Nissi*, the Lord our Banner/Victory. The Lord that heals, *Jehovah Rophe*, may have healed a sickness in your life. These times need to be documented.

In this age of computers, we are told to always make a back up disk of anything we are doing on the computer. The reason for this is so that if a power outage occurs, and we lose what we were working on at the computer, we don't have to start back at the beginning. We simply use our back up disk and start again where we left off.

Sometimes in our Christian walk, we have spiritual blackouts or valleys – what do we do then? Do we start back at the beginning? No, we simply go to the altar to receive encouragement from how God has worked in our life in the past. Then we can go forward again in our walk with the Lord.

The word *altar* comes from the Hebrew word *mizbeah*, which means a raised place where a sacrifice was made.[8] When God touches your life in a special and mighty way, you are in a raised place spiritually, poised to make a sacrifice of praise and worship.

There are two types of altars mentioned in the Bible.

One is a sacrificial altar on which burnt offerings were made to God for forgiveness of sins. This kind of altar was realized in Jesus Christ, the perfect Lamb of God, when He sacrificed His life for our sins at the cross. Because of Jesus' death, we no longer offer burnt offerings on an altar to God. Our sins were covered at Calvary.

The word altar comes from the Hebrew word mizbeah, which means a raised place where a sacrifice was made.[8] When God touches your life in a special and mighty way, you are in a raised place spiritually, poised to make a sacrifice of praise and worship.

Because of Jesus' death, we no longer offer burnt offerings on an altar to God. Our sins were covered at Calvary.

The second type of altar in the Bible is an altar built in remembrance and praise of a spiritual experience with the Lord. When God called Abram by faith to take his family and go wherever God would lead him, Abram obeyed.

Read Genesis 12:2-7. What did God say, and how did Abram respond?

_____

_____

_____

The second type of altar in the Bible is an altar built in remembrance and praise of a spiritual experience with the Lord.

Abram, Jacob, Moses, and Gideon all experienced God in an incredible and personal way. To celebrate those moments, they each built an altar.

Read Genesis 35:1-7. What did God do that Jacob was commemorating?

_____

_____

Read Exodus 17:10-15. How did Jehovah God become *The LORD my Banner* to Moses and Joshua? _____

_____

_____

Read Judges 6:1-24. Describe Gideon's situation and how he experienced God in a special way. _____

_____

_____

Abram, Jacob, Moses, and Gideon all experienced God in an incredible and personal way. To celebrate those moments, they each built an altar.

I love to read the psalms because we can see into David's innermost feelings about the Lord. Being honest about who we are and our relationship with the Lord is part of building an altar to God. Altars are intimate and quiet places, personal testimonies to the Lord of your experiences with Him. An altar also provides a place to go back to in worship when you reach a dry spot or valley in your walk with the Lord. You don't have to go back to the beginning of the relationship, you just go back to that last special time of worship and fellowship with God.

Altars also act as reminders to confirm for us that something really *did* happen and document our encounter with God. Altars prevent the enemy from distorting the truth by telling us that we were just emotional or that nothing really happened. God moves mightily in our lives healing, comforting, directing, saving, delivering, and more!

Fill in the blanks:

• Psalm 7:17: *I will give* _____ *to the* LORD *because of righteousness and will sing* _____ *to the name of the* LORD *Most High.*

• Isaiah 19:19: *In that day there will be an* _____ *to the* LORD *in the heart of Egypt, and a* _____ *to the* LORD *at its border.*

• Psalm 40:2: *He* _____ *me out of the slimy pit, out of the mud and mire; he set my feet on a rock and gave me a* _____ *place to stand.*

• Psalm 26:6-7: *I wash my hands in innocence, and go about your* _____ *O* LORD, *proclaiming aloud your praise and* _____ *of all your wonderful deeds.*

• Psalm 43:4: *Then will I go to the* _____ *to God, my joy and my delight. I will praise you with the harp, O God, my God.*

Build an altar. Spend time in praise and worship with the Lord for what He has done in your life and for who He is – your Father, your heavenly Daddy who loves you so and is always, always, always there for you. Tell Him you love Him, and thank Him for the miracles in your life.

Keep a spiral notebook or journal of prayers. When you need to "build an altar," mark the date and write out your prayer to God. Write what's in your heart. This is only between you and your Father. You might write in this journal daily, monthly, or yearly. Do whatever God leads you to do. Periodically go back and read your entries. Remember, this altar is like a back up disk for you. (God doesn't forget or get confused like we do.) You will be amazed at how your faith will be strengthened when you begin to make a written record of the times God moved in your life in mighty ways. You will know that you know that you know that He does. Build an altar to God starting today.

Being honest about who we are and our relationship with the Lord is part of building an altar to God. Altars are intimate and quiet places, personal testimonies to the Lord of your experiences with Him.

TRUTHS TO EMBRACE

_____

_____

_____

_____

_____

_____

Week 8

BUT MY DAD CAN

My husband, Bruce, is a wonderful dad. He loves his children dearly, and that love and devotion is evident to everyone around him. I have watched the Lord bring several men into Bruce's life who were not very interested in their children. But as Bruce spent time with these men, I saw God change their attitudes and priorities toward their children, without any pressure from Bruce. These men saw what a precious relationship they were missing. They saw children who knew unconditional love from their father. They saw a father who made time to spend with his children. They saw a father whose greatest joy was his children. And they saw children who could climb up on their father's lap hurt, crying, dirty, or celebrating. As the desire for a similar relationship grew inside these men, their past priorities and selfish wants seemed of less value.

This week we will explore our relationship with our heavenly Daddy. As we grow in our relationship with Him, our fleshly desires will diminish so that we can truly become His effective ministers of reconciliation. Believers and unbelievers that we meet will be drawn to the Lord because of the precious relationship with our Father that they see through our responses, actions, and words.

DAY 1
Healer of My Hurts

DAY 2
He Leads, I Follow

DAY 3
Battle of the Wills

DAY 4
Enough Is Enough

DAY 5
Daddy's Lap

Week Eight, Day One

HEALER OF MY HURTS

I will repay you for the years the locusts have eaten — the great locust and the young locust, the other locusts and the locust swarm – my great army that I sent among you.

Joel 2:25

When my children were young, they ran to me to fix their hurts. Often it just took a simple mother's kiss to make everything right with the world again. Sometimes it took a little more. I would pull them up on my lap, hold them, kiss them, and lovingly rock their troubles away. It never occurred to them to run to someone else. They had complete trust in my ability and my faithful desire to heal their hurts.

As children of God, we have the same avenue open to us. We have a heavenly Father who has the ability and the desire to heal all of our hurts more completely than any loving parent ever could. Our only hindrance to healing is running to someone or something else to fix it instead of going straight to *Jehovah-Rophe*, The Lord who Heals.

Read Exodus 15:22-27. This is the first time in Scripture that God refers to Himself as our healer. How was the water described? _____

_____

_____

Has there ever been a relationship in your life that was a bitter drink to swallow? When? _____

_____

_____

What did Moses do to fix the water problem? _____

_____

I once co-chaired a committee with a very strong-willed and controlling woman who brought bitterness and division to every meeting. It seemed as though her goals in life were to do the opposite of anything I suggested and to prevent any cohesiveness in our group.

I did my best to anticipate her next move and maneuver around it. I prayed for God to change her. I even prayed for God to remove her from our group. What I didn't

As children of God, we have a heavenly Father who has the ability and the desire to heal all of our hurts more completely than any loving parent ever could.

do was follow Moses' lead and simply cry out to God for help, giving Him both the problem and the solution. I was crying for God to just fix her. I even gave Him two choices: change her or remove her. I thought I was being very open and flexible. After all, I am a team player. *But healing never happens when I throw my own remedy stick into the bitter waters of Marah.* God chose a third solution. His choice was to begin to heal the situation by exposing *my* sin. I did not love this woman unconditionally with His love. I had not forgiven her. Her actions had been wrong, but so had my lack of love and unforgiveness. I've learned that for healing to occur in a relationship, God usually starts with changing me first.

I've learned that for healing to occur in a relationship, God usually starts with changing me first.

What does verse 26 tell us God requires of us?_____
_____
_____

In the following scriptures, what does God command us to do?

Mark 11:25 _____
_____

Mark 12:20-31 _____
_____

Does God give us any exceptions for forgiving someone who has hurt us deeply?
Yes_____ No_____

If we follow God's commands, what has He promised to do for us (Exo. 15:26)?
_____
_____

Give Him your hurts so that He can heal your bitterness. Then you can truly drink of His living waters.

Joyce Meyer says that we can either be bitter or get better.

It is your choice, your decision, an act of your will. If you are nursing your hurts, it is because you have chosen to be bitter and sick instead of letting *Jehovah-Rophe* heal you. The only thing that stops Him from healing you is yourself.

Beloved, let go of the anger or bitterness onto which you are holding so tightly – even if you have to ask Jesus to pry open your hands and take them from you. The main thing is to give Him your hurts so that He can heal your bitterness. Then you can truly drink of His living waters.

Read John 5:1-15.

Fill in the blanks from John 5:6: *When Jesus saw him lying there and learned that he had been in this condition for a long time, He asked him, "Do you _____ to get_____?"*

The phrase *he had been* is translated from the Greek word, *echo*, which means to hold, to have possession of the mind, to cling to, or to be closely joined to a thing.[1]

As we learned earlier in this study, very often our hurts become our identity. We hold on to them too tightly. Perhaps this is why Jesus asked this man if he wanted to get well. Many people today have unreconciled relationships simply because they choose to hold on to their victim mentality and refuse to let go of the hurt.

Many people today have unreconciled relationships simply because they choose to hold on to their victim mentality and refuse to let go of the hurt.

What was the man's excuse for not trying to get healed in the past?_____
_____
_____

What are our excuses for the hurts onto which we are still holding? _____
_____
_____

Read Acts 3:1-10.

What did the crippled man do every day? _____
_____

How long had he been crippled? _____

What did he want from Peter and John? _____
_____

What did they give him instead? _____
_____

This man had been crippled since birth. We are no different. When we have a broken relationship, unforgiveness, bitterness, or anger, we are crippled from the time we give birth to that sin. Make no mistake, we may have been the victims, but our reaction to the hurt is sin. Remember what we learned in an earlier lesson: forgiving someone does not mean that they were right and you were wrong. They may have been very wrong, but forgiveness is about *your* heart attitude and following God's command for *your* life.

This man in the account in Acts sat daily begging at the gate called Beautiful, the most populated entrance to the Temple. How many of us sit for all to see, looking like spiritual paupers or beggars because of the hurts we have allowed to cripple us?

Several years ago, I had a very real burden to pray for our ladies' retreat. The week before, I cleared my calendar just to have time to pray. Three days before the retreat, as I was on my knees, God showed me a picture of a large cross. At the base of the cross were acres of drawstring brown bags that were all the same size. I couldn't see any ground because the bags touched each other and went as far as my eyes could see. For three more days I prayed, and each day I had the same vision. Finally, I questioned the Lord because I didn't quite understand. I said, *Lord, I understand that these bags represent the spiritual baggage or strongholds that the women are carrying, but the bags are all the same size and look the same. Some of the women coming this weekend are carrying some really big hurts, and some have smaller hurts. Why do all the bags look the same?* My Lord replied, *My child, they are all the same to Me. You are the ones who rank hurts and sin, not Me.*

All God desires is for us to give Him our hurts, our sin, and allow Him to be our *Jehovah-Rophe*, The Lord who Heals.

Look back over Acts 3:5-6 and fill in the blanks.

The man gave them his attention, _____ to get something from them.

Then Peter said, " _____ or _____ I do not have, but what I have I give you. In the name of _____ _____ of Nazareth, walk."

We waste so much time expecting others to fix us. What silver or gold do you want to make you well? Is it an apology? Is it for "them" to pay for what they did to "me"? Is it justice? Is it sympathy from those who see you sitting crippled at the gate Beautiful of your life? Do you want your offender to become an outcast, hated by all that see your hurt? Is the silver or gold you seek having that person somehow make it up to you for what they did or said?

These are unrealistic expectations. Only God can fill the voids and heal our hurts. Anything else is just a band-aid. Had the beggar just received silver or gold, he would have returned the next day to beg for more silver and gold just to make it through the day. Instead, he received true healing from the Lord, the kind of healing that goes to the root of the problem and fills the void.

Forgiving someone does not mean that they were right and you were wrong.

Forgiveness is about your heart attitude and following God's command for your life.

What was the man's response to the healing that made him whole? _____

_____

Read Hebrews 12:1-4 and write out verse 4. _____

_____

If you are still struggling with hurts, unforgiveness, anger, or bitterness and are expecting someone to fix you, it is time to recognize that you are struggling with sin, because you, like the lame man, are trying to buy healing with silver and gold. Your healing was bought and paid for at the cross by the shed blood of Christ Jesus. Don't let it be in vain! It is time to quit being crippled beggars at the gate. Start walking in victory. Now is the time to let Jesus do what He longs to do, and praise His name!

According to Acts 3:10, after the healing power of Jesus, how did people view the lame man? _____

_____

_____

_____

This is the ministry of reconciliation – that those around us would see something different about us because of the Lord Jesus Christ in our life, and as a result, will want what we have. No one wants to be without hope like the crippled beggar. What people do want is a God who can heal hurts and reconcile relationships when there is no other possible way.

Write out Joel 2:25 in your own words. If you have a specific hurt that you need to release, personalize this verse with your name and specific situation, and then stand on that promise. This is *Jehovah-Rophe's* promise to you that He can fill the void from your hurts.

_____

_____

_____

_____

_____

_____

TRUTHS TO EMBRACE

_____

_____

_____

_____

_____

_____

Week Eight, Day Two
HE LEADS, I FOLLOW

Some trust in chariots and some in horses, but we trust in the name of the LORD our God.

Psalm 20:7

Because I know my God and His character, I know that He is trustworthy.

A woman in one of my Bible studies once confided in me about some serious marital problems she was experiencing. When she told her husband she had talked with me, he was very upset. He was a very private person and did not want the details of the situation to become public knowledge. He called and asked to meet with me. After we were introduced, the first thing that he said to me was, "I don't know you. I don't know what you might do with this information because I don't know what kind of person you are. I know my wife knows you and obviously trust you, but I have just met you." I could understand his concern. We had no history together. He knew nothing of my character, my beliefs, or my standards. As time passed, he came to trust me because I "proved" myself through my commitment to keeping their confidence, along with my compassionate concern for his wife.

I have a history with my God. I have experienced His trustworthiness over and over in my life. I have lived His Word so that I know that He is trustworthy. I have seen Him work through the lives of other believers. Scripture tells me that I can trust Him and His precepts, and I know from experience and by faith that is true. We have a relationship. We spend time together. Because I know my God and His character, I know that He is trustworthy.

Read Jeremiah 7:8, Jeremiah 48:7, Isaiah 2:22, and Job 15:31.

Name some things in which we put our trust other than Father God. _____
_____
_____

What can be the outcome of trusting these things?_____
_____

I can tell you why I trust God, but those are just my words, my experiences, and my opinions. Let's look to the Word of God for the absolute truth about why God is worthy of trust.

Look up the following scriptures and explain what each teaches about why you can trust God.

2 Samuel 7:28 _____

_____

Nahum 1:7 _____

_____

Jeremiah 49:11 _____

_____

Jeremiah 39:18 _____

_____

Psalm 19:7 _____

_____

Psalm 111:7 _____

_____

Psalm 112:7 _____

_____

Psalm 119:138 _____

_____

Psalm 22:4-5 _____

_____

Hebrews 13:8 _____

_____

According to Romans 15:13, what is the outcome of trusting God? _____

_____

_____

Read John 14:1 and fill in the blanks.

Jesus said, "Do not let your hearts be troubled. Trust in _____; trust also in _____."

The Greek word translated here as *trust* is *pisteuo,* meaning to place confidence in.[2]

According to John 14:5-12, how can we know what the Father is like?_____

_____

How can we know what Jesus is like? _____

_____

The word translated *believe* in verses 10-11 and the word translated *faith* in verse 12 are actually this same Greek word *pisteuo* meaning to trust or to put confidence in.[3]

Reread John 14:5-12 and substitute the word *trust* for *believe* and *faith*. How does this change your view of the Father? Of Jesus? _____

_____

_____

_____

Read the following scriptures and write the truth of God's Word about the character, heart, and passion of Jesus. Because of this, why can you trust Him?

John 6:35 _____

John 10:11 _____

John 10:27 _____

Luke 5:24 _____

Luke 4:36 _____

Luke 5:32 _____

Luke 19:10 _____

Read Luke 15:3-7.

The shepherd lives with his flock. He protects his sheep from animals and dangers that would harm or prey on them. In fact, he will daily risk his life to take care of his sheep. He guides them by day and sleeps with them at night. They are totally dependent on their shepherd; he provides for all their needs.

Sometimes if the shepherd has an unruly lamb, he will break its legs so it cannot run off anymore. Then he will lovingly place the lamb on his shoulders and carry it at all times until it is well. In this way, the lamb experiences intimate love and contact with his shepherd. The lamb learns that it can and should trust the shepherd in every aspect of its life.

It must break the shepherd's heart to have to discipline the lamb in such a way, but in his agape love he is actively seeking the highest good of the lamb. He can only protect and guide the lamb when it stays in the flock. The lamb faces all kinds of dangers when it wanders away from the shepherd's able care. How much more pain would there be if the lamb wandered off and was attacked by a wolf?

I trust God because I know Him from experience.

In John 10:14-15, how did Jesus describe Himself? _____
_____

Read Acts 12. What did Peter realize (verse 11)? _____
_____

We are called to trust God because He has demonstrated His power to us through miracles.

Isn't that just like us?! We say we are trusting God, but then we don't recognize His hand on our life until later because we really don't expect Him to come through for us.

God has convicted me many times about my lip service. Too many times I have said, "I'm trusting God, but…"

There is no room for disclaimers in our walk with the Lord. You need to know, say, and believe, "I am trusting God, period!" Why? Because He alone is worthy of your trust.

Read John 14:9-11. In verse 9 we read that Jesus said, *"Anyone who has seen Me has seen the Father."* The phrase *has seen* is translated from the Greek word *horao,* meaning to become acquainted with by experience.[4] I trust God because I know Him from experience.

In John 14:11, we are called to trust God because He has demonstrated His power to us through miracles. What greater miracles can we ask for than to see God's hand on our life over time? When we look back, how can we not trust Him with our future, our family, our friends, our relationships, and our church?

Write out a time when you didn't completely trust God but as you look back, you see His hand on the situation. Praise Him for that miracle. _____
_____
_____
_____

In Acts 12, in whom did Herod put his trust? _____

In whom did Peter put his trust?_____

Re-read Romans 15:13. How do you know Paul was trusting Jesus with his life?

_____

_____

_____

Read Psalm 3. Does this remind you of the story of Peter and Herod? What similarities do you see? _____

_____

_____

_____

What a comfort to see how David trusted God with his life and the retribution against his enemies. Peter did the same thing and God's trustworthy nature was faithful.

When my children were young, I could control most of their world. I chose their clothes, their food, their friends, their entertainment, and their living environment. As a young mother and an immature Christian, it was difficult for me to totally trust them to the Lord. Small children are completely dependent on their parents, and I wanted to be sure they were protected and taken care of the way I wanted. My lack of completely trusting them to the Lord was a sin. Who was I to think that I was more loving and able than God?

As my children have grown into teenagers and young married adults, it has become very easy to trust them to the Lord. My finite parenting skills are flagrant. I can't be with them every moment – but He can. I don't know their thoughts and plans – but He does. I can't make them see truth – but He can. I can't protect them – or worse yet, I might protect them from the lesson that their Father God wants to teach them – but His plans for them are perfect. I can't fix them – but He can and does. The truth found in Romans 15:13 is that my peace and my joy are to know that my children are in the hands of the Father and that He loves them more than I could. More important, through our relationship, His Word, the faith He has given me, and the miracles He has done in my life, He has assured me that He is completely trustworthy. (Not to mention the fact that He always does a better job than I do!)

Read Acts 4:1-20.

What happened to Peter and John for teaching about Jesus? _____

_____

_____

When we worry, it is because we don't trust God with that situation or person.

According to verses 8-12 and verses 19-20, what did Peter do immediately after spending the night in jail for teaching about Jesus? _____

_____

_____

According to verse 13, where did Peter and John find the courage and conviction to trust Jesus with the direction of their lives and the consequences? _____

_____

_____

Read Acts 14:19-20.

When you truly trust Him, you must trust Him with both the problem and the solution, or you do not really trust Him at all!

Do you think Paul had the same kind of trust as Peter and John? Explain. _____

_____

_____

What are some other scriptures to confirm your conclusion? _____

_____

_____

Read Luke 12:22-34.

In verse 24, how did Jesus describe your worth to the Father? _____

_____

_____

_____

When we worry, it is because we don't trust God with that situation or person. My friend says that worry is the sin of unbelief and that it says one of two things about what we believe about God: (1) He is not big enough to handle the situation, or (2) He doesn't care enough to do it.

Read Psalm 20:7.

In what chariots and horses have you trusted?_____

_____

_____

Is there a situation or a person you need to give to the loving and trusted care of your Shepherd, *Jehovah Rohi*? _____

_____

_____

_____

Remember, when you truly trust Him, you must trust Him with both the problem and the solution, or you do not really trust Him at all!

What keeps you from totally trusting the Lord with everything and everyone in your life? The problem is not with God's capability. Many of the broken relationships and problems in life are caused because we try to fix someone or something instead of trusting God to handle it in His way and in His time. It is much easier and much safer to just give it to God and let Him handle it. He is *Jehovah Rohi*, the Lord our Shepherd.

TRUTHS TO EMBRACE

_____

_____

_____

_____

_____

_____

BATTLE OF THE WILLS

If the Lord delights in a man's way, he makes his steps firm.

Psalm 37:23

One of the biggest stumbling blocks to accepting the sovereignty of God is trying to reconcile the concept of free will. The truths that God is sovereign and that He has given us a free will both work perfectly together. Conflict comes when we try to figure the concepts with our finite minds. These truths can only be completely reconciled in the infinite mind of our God. The bottom line is that we must trust Him by faith.

The truths that God is sovereign and that He has given us a free will both work perfectly together.

Read Romans 9:19-29. Then read this portion of it from the Message Bible, below.

> *Are you going to object, "So how can God blame us for anything since He's in charge of everything? If the big decisions are already made, what say do we have in it?" Who in the world do you think you are to second-guess God? Do you for one moment suppose any of us knows enough to call God into question? Clay doesn't talk back to the fingers that mold it saying, "Why did you shape me like this?" Isn't it obvious that a potter has a perfect right to shape one lump of clay into a vase for holding flowers and another into a pot for cooking beans? If God needs one style of pottery especially designed to show His angry displeasure and another style carefully crafted to show His glorious goodness, isn't that all right? Either or both happens to Jews, but it also happens to the other people.*

What does Isaiah 55:8-9 say?_____

_____

_____

_____

Webster's dictionary defines the word *sovereign* as "above or superior to all others; supreme in power, rank, or authority; independent of all others."[5]

Read Genesis 1:1, and fill in the blank: *In the beginning* _____.

Did God need help creating the world or did He exercise supreme authority and unlimited power? Why? _____

_____

_____

The first name that our sovereign Lord uses to refer to Himself is *God*. In fact, He uses this name for Himself over 2,700 times in the Old Testament. This is the Hebrew word, *Elohim*, which means "the one true God."[6] In his book, *The Names of God*, Nathan Stone describes *Elohim*, "There is blessing and comfort in this great name of God signifying supreme power, sovereignty, and glory on the one hand… and on the other hand signifying a covenant relationship which He is ever faithful to keep."[7]

Read Jeremiah 16:21 and Ezekiel 13:20-23. Why does our sovereign Lord wield His power in our lives and the life of our nation? _____

_____

Read Romans 13:1-2 and Titus 3:1.

Who establishes governments and rulers? _____

_____

In China and Russia, there are very real obstacles to worshipping Jesus Christ. Yet amazingly, Christianity is on the rise in these countries.

How are we to respond to non-Christian government leaders?_____

_____

According to Acts 4:27-28, who put Pontius Pilate and Herod into office?

_____

How did this affect Christianity? _____

_____

Read Romans 9:17.

Who put Pharaoh into power? Why? _____

_____

_____

Do you think that the children of Israel experienced a different relationship with God because they lived in a country ruled by Pharaoh? Why? Do you think they understood this at the time? Explain. _____

_____

_____

Read Daniel 4. Look close at verse 17. To what extent is God willing to go for us to know and accept that He is sovereign?_____

_____

_____

_____

In reality, do you think that He was just trying to be mean to Nebuchadnezzar?

_____

Through this experience, a cruel, self-righteous, pagan king came to know and accept God as his one true God. As the leader of this nation, many others followed his lead and also came to worship the one true, sovereign *Elohim*. In our world today, we are able to worship freely in the United States. However, Christianity is on the decline in our nation. In China and Russia, there are very real obstacles to worshipping Jesus Christ. Yet amazingly, Christianity is on the rise in these countries. We Americans often self-righteously think everyone should have our type of government and religious opportunities. Could it be that these opportunities sometimes become obstacles to our walk with the Lord, and that God in His great mercy and sovereignty has allowed pagan, sometimes cruel leadership in a nation so that His people are brought closer to Him and His glory?

Recently a friend of mine asked me to pray for her niece. She was not a Christian and had been sent to Russia on a job assignment. Her family was worried about her and how she would be influenced in that country. Perhaps our sovereign God arranged for her to go there and placed her in just the circumstances needed for her to come to know Him.

Read Proverbs 21:1. In this verse, Scripture is talking about a pagan king. What is the promise from a sovereign God for us to stand on? _____

_____

_____

_____

Write out Genesis 50:20. _____

_____

_____

• The word *intended* is translated from the Hebrew word, *chashab,* meaning to weave or fabricate, to plot or contrive, or to think, plan, or calculate. It also refers to craftsmen "inventing" instruments of music and weapons of war.[8]

• The word *lives* is translated from the Hebrew word, *chayah,* meaning to live prosperously, to live forever, or to be restored to life or health.[9]

• The word *many* is translated from the Hebrew word, *rab,* meaning many or abundant.[10]

Now, taking into consideration these Hebrew meanings, rewrite Genesis 50:20 in your own words. _____

_____

_____

_____

Joseph understood and trusted in a sovereign God.

Joseph understood and trusted in a sovereign God. He focused on God through his trials, instead of on his circumstances. Too often in my life when someone has hurt me, my focus has been on that hurt. Instead, I need to focus on the sovereignty of God and His plan to use this situation in my life. Sometimes He engineers adverse circumstances or personal hurts in my life to teach me, to hone me, or just for His divine master plan – reasons that I may not understand at the time. When these situations arise, I need to ask Him, *What do You want to teach me here?* and then forgive the person who hurt me before bitterness takes root.

Joseph could have become a very angry, bitter man at his brothers and at God. Instead, he lived a life of forgiveness and meekness. Meekness does not mean being a doormat – it is strength under control, and a quiet trust in the sovereignty of God no matter what the situation. Meekness is the opposite of self-interest and self-assertiveness. Meekness means seeing beyond our own feelings and focusing on God.

Meekness means seeing beyond our own feelings and focusing on God.

According to Psalm 37:11, what is the consequence of being meek? _____

_____

_____

Read Jeremiah 1:4-12. How would you describe God's sovereignty in Jeremiah's life? _____

_____

Read Proverbs 19:21 and 16:9. Describe a time in your life when you had a certain plan, but God directed your steps elsewhere. When was that time? What was the outcome? _____

_____

Read Acts 22:1-21. What was Paul's plan for his own life? _____

_____

What was God's plan for Paul's life? _____

_____

When you are in a situation that seems to be hopelessly straying from your own plan, you can stand on the promise in Romans 4:20-21.

Fill in the blanks.

God had (and has) *the* _____ *to do what He had* _____.

Paul seemed to be determined in his life plan; however, our sovereign God had a different idea. Paul was a very strong-willed person, but God's will is stronger. Paul was not the first, nor will he be the last, to enter into a battle of wills with God. But no matter how hard we may fight Him, the outcome is always the same.

Paul was not the first, nor will he be the last, to enter into a battle of wills with God.

In Proverbs 21:30, what does God promise will be the outcome of our battle of wills? _____
_____
_____

Let's do a quick study of the "I wills" between God and Pharaoh.

Fill in the blanks.

God	Pharaoh
Exodus 6:6: *I will* _____ _____	Exodus 5:2: *I will* _____ _____

In Exodus 9:28, what did Pharaoh promise Moses? _____
_____
_____

Moses did what Pharaoh asked, but what did he see in Pharaoh's heart? _____
_____
_____

In Exodus 9:35-36, what did Pharaoh do as soon as his circumstance changed?
_____
_____

God's statement, "I will," is based on His character which never changes.

Pharaoh's statement, "I will," was an emotional reaction to his circumstances. In fact, it took three more plagues before he even let the Israelites leave Egypt. Then he changed his mind and sent troops after them. God's statement, "I will," is based on His character which never changes. Pharaoh considered himself all-powerful, yet our sovereign God had the first and the last word. The children of Israel may have thought God was losing the battle. But what they did not see or understand was God's big picture. We have the same problem. Too often we don't see God's hand in our circumstances because we are seeing with our limited vision.

The children of Israel may have thought God was losing the battle. But what they did not see or understand was God's big picture.

According to Exodus 9:13, why did God bring the Israelites out of bondage in Egypt? _____

_____

In Exodus 3:12, what is God's promise to us? _____

_____

God brings us out of bondage so that we can worship Him unhindered. Like the Israelites, we lose our focus, believing God has delivered us just so that we could live in the Promised Land. Instead, God will be sovereign in our lives to bring us closer to Him, not just to improve our circumstances.

As I look back over my life, I realize that I have experienced troubled relationships and a lack of peace and joy in my own life because I did not trust God's sovereignty. I have experienced turmoil while trying to fix this or that when I really needed to wait on God and move in faith, knowing that He has the situation under control.

Too often we don't see God's hand in our circumstances because we are seeing with our limited vision.

What did Moses tell the Israelites in Exodus 14:13-14?_____

_____

What was God's response in Exodus 14:15-18? _____

_____

_____

Re-read Psalm 20:7.

Pharaoh thought he could "will" his own way, trusting in his horses and chariots, but the result was death.

Write out Proverbs 14:12._____

_____

_____

What incredible peace I have when I simply turn the situation over to the Lord and say, I know You are sovereign, so I will trust You, even though I don't understand.

When I decide to fix a situation by "my will," I risk my peace, my joy, or the health of a relationship. What incredible peace I have when I simply turn the situation over to the Lord and say, *I know You are sovereign, so I will trust You, even though I don't understand.* Is there something or someone you need to give over to God's plan? Give it to Him today and ask Him to make "your will" into "His will," and then bask in His peace.

TRUTHS TO EMBRACE

_____

_____

_____

_____

_____

_____

ENOUGH IS ENOUGH

The Lord will reply to them: "I am sending you grain, new wine and oil, enough to satisfy you fully; never again will I make you an object of scorn to the nations."

Joel 2:19

The longer I walk with the Lord, the more I become aware of my own lack and His sufficiency.

The longer I walk with the Lord, the more I become aware of my own lack and His sufficiency. He is *I Am Enough*. He is our *Jehovah Sufficient*. He is the God who is personal, continuous, absolute, and enough. Nothing else is required to fill our needs except Him. To say that God is sufficient doesn't seem like a big enough word to describe Him, yet that is exactly what He is. He is perfect for our every need. Webster's dictionary defines *sufficient* as "enough to meet the needs of a situation or a proposed end."[11]

After I had my last child, I began to gain weight. When I was sad, mad, bored, or stressed, I headed to the pantry for comfort. This addiction and bondage was awful because that candy or that cookie never filled the void or need I was experiencing. I was miserable. Twelve years later I finally allowed God to be enough to meet my needs. What freedom came to my heart! He alone could fill in those places without my feeling miserable and overstuffed!

We look for all kinds of things to fill the hurt and empty places of our lives. It may be cars, boats, vacations, big houses, food, relationships, movies, or even clothes, but none of these things ever satisfy. Many of us are in financial and spiritual bondage because we have had too much of the wrong things. The good news is that we don't have to continue in this sin and bondage because we serve a God who truly is enough.

The book of Joel was written during the time of the divided kingdom. The prophet Joel wrote to the southern kingdom of Judah. In the first part of his book, Joel warned the people of the coming devastation from a swarm of locusts that would fall upon the land as a result of their sin and disobedience.

When locusts descend on an area, they look like a dark cloud settling upon the earth. Sometimes there can be up to 80 million of them over an area as large as several hundred kilometers. They devour every piece of vegetation in sight, leaving a pathway of total devastation.

For Christians, sin and strongholds in our lives can have the same effect.

The times when:

> The devastation seems too much,
>
> The hurt seems too deep,
>
> The sin seems too great,
>
> The problem seems overwhelming, or
>
> The situation seems irreconcilable

are the times when we must look through God's eyes and claim His promises, because when we look with our human eyes of reason, we will miss Him every time.

Read Joel 2:12-19. What did God command us to do in verse 12? _____

_____

_____

_____

Too often, we know in our minds that God is sufficient, but our feelings tell us otherwise.

The Hebrew word translated *heart* is *lebab*, meaning the inner man, heart, will, understanding, memory, emotions, or determination.[12]

Too often, we know in our minds that God is sufficient, but our feelings tell us otherwise. The reality is that our feelings and emotions will lie to us. We must stand on the promises that we know, regardless of our feelings.

In verse 13, what does the LORD our God ask us to give Him? _____

_____

The people of that day tore their clothes as an outward sign of remorse, but God is looking for inner repentance.

According to verse 14, if we do what He asks, how will He bless us? _____

_____

_____

In verse 16, what was the command for the assembly? _____

_____

_____

We need to consecrate, or dedicate, our hurts, anger, disappointments, and broken relationships to the Lord and then prayerfully place them on His altar of sacrifice.

Verse 18 reads, *Then the Lord will be jealous* _____ *His land and take pity on His people.*

Our jealous God is not looking down at you from heaven with His hands on His hips saying, "Well, you got what you deserved because you desired something more than Me." No, He is jealous for you. He is actively seeking your highest good with His agape love.

Our jealous God is not looking down at you from heaven with His hands on His hips saying, "Well, you got what you deserved because you desired something more than Me." No, He is jealous for you. He is actively seeking your highest good with His agape love. He wants the best for you. He wants to fill in your hurts, anger, disappointments, voids, and broken relationships with Himself, because only He is enough to satisfy you fully.

Write out verse 19. _____
_____
_____
_____
_____

God was sending the people everything they needed to recover from the devastation brought by the locusts. What did He send?

- **Grain** – Our need, for which God provides
- **New Wine** – Our salvation
- **Oil** – Used to consecrate something for sacred use, our healing and restoration of our repentant heart by the Holy Spirit

I have a great need to discuss things. I like to talk things out; sometimes I need to say the same thing several times, as I work through it. Sharing my heart and having someone else share theirs is the way I perceive love and closeness. However, men usually are more concise. My husband, Bruce, likes to have everything down on paper, preferably in bulleted form. He only needs to say or hear something once and then he is done. He is also very private and not emotional. We are total opposites – and this brings balance to our marriage.

Early in our marriage, I spent many hours being angry with Bruce because he did not fill my need to talk and express my feelings verbally. Finally, I gave my expectations for having an in-depth conversation with Bruce to the Lord and asked Him to be my grain, new wine, and oil in that area of my life and marriage. What freedom! And what a difference it made in my marriage! I was able to love and accept Bruce without strings, because God was enough for me in that area. God listens attentively to me as I pour my heart out to Him for as long as I want or need.

A friend once gave me a basket with a bag of grain, a bottle of wine, and a bottle of oil. This basket is my physical reminder that God is sufficient for all my needs.

Many things can cause voids in our lives:
- Financial insecurity
- Unreconciled relationships

- A childhood lost due to abuse
- Death of a loved one
- Divorce, or just a bad marriage
- An unsaved spouse

But when we expect any other things besides God to fill all the voids of our lives, we need to repent of the sin of idolatry.

Read Hosea 7:13-14.

Woe to them, because they have strayed from Me!
Straying from God is looking for people or things to fill the void that only God can fill. Straying from God is looking for the wrong "fix" to the problem instead of asking God to reveal the root of the problem.

Destruction to them, because they have rebelled against Me!
Rebellion is idolatry when we are looking for someone or some thing to fill the place of God.

I long to redeem them, but they speak lies against Me.
Have you ever said that you have prayed about something that you have given to God, but He hasn't changed anything? Often we offer things to Him with our options on how we want Him to solve them. Until we give Him the problem *and* the solution, we haven't really given it to Him to work healing in our life, or the life of someone for which we are praying.

They do not cry out to Me from their hearts, but wail upon their beds.
Wailing on our bed is simply lip service if there is no change of heart or repentance. We have to trust God to be enough. If we worry or try to fix something, then we don't trust God.

They gathered together for grain and new wine, but turn away from Me.
Do you notice what's missing here? What about the oil? They wanted salvation and blessing, but turned away when it came to having their hearts healed and restored by the Holy Spirit through repentance and trust. We need to get rid of the "bless me" mentality! God may not change our circumstance, or heal us the way we desire; but He will be enough to satisfy us fully!

We need to respond and not react to circumstances and sin. When we react, we look for a superficial fix to a situation, a band-aid. It is saying to God, *This is what I want You to do.* But God is not a catalog from which to order. He is a holy, righteous God who desires our hearts. When we respond, when we give God the problem *and* the

Straying from God is looking for people or things to fill the void that only God can fill.

God is not a catalog from which to order. He is a holy, righteous God who desires our hearts.

solution, we seek the root of the problem *and* trust God to be enough – no matter what!

Go back to Joel 2 and read verses 20-23. In verse 23, what does God promise to send us? _____

_____

_____

The Lord takes the barren places of our lives and makes them productive.

In Joel 2:24-25, what does the Lord promise? _____

_____

_____

He doesn't change the past, but He fills the void, heals the hurts, and changes the way we deal with the present and the future.

What does verse 26 tell us the Lord works for us? _____

_____

_____

The word translated *wonders* is the Hebrew word, *pala*, meaning to be surpassing, to be beyond one's power, to be difficult to understand, wonderful.[13] Beloved, when your sufficient God fills in those places, it will surpass your expectations because His work is so wonderful and complete.

Read Joel 2:27-32. What does God promise us? _____

_____

_____

_____

Read 2 Corinthians 1:3-11 and fill in the blanks.

He _____ delivered us from such a deadly peril, and He_____ delivers us. On Him we have set our hope that He will _____t o deliver us.

Webster's dictionary defines *deliver* as, "to give birth, to rescue, to send to an intended destination."[14] Jesus came to give hope to the hopeless and to set the captives free. He came to deliver us.

What is our promise in John 8:36?_____

In Romans 6:18? _____

Read John 14:8-14. What did Philip ask of Jesus? _____
_____

How did Jesus respond? _____
_____

Isn't that just like us? We have everything we need in Jesus, yet we miss it and keep looking for something else to fill in those places. Spend some time pondering these questions today. What in your heart do you need to render to God today? Where are you not letting Him be enough? Where are you trying to fill the void with other things? Will you respond and not react to His desire to deliver you today, and let Him be the grain, new wine, and oil enough to satisfy you fully?

TRUTHS TO EMBRACE

_____
_____
_____
_____
_____
_____

Week Eight, Day Five

DADDY'S LAP

Say to the Israelites: "I am the Lord, and I will bring you out from under the yoke of the Egyptians. I will free you from being slaves to them, and I will redeem you with an out-stretched arm and with mighty acts of judgment."

Exodus 6:6

I would rather be in His presence in the wilderness than without Him in the Promised Land.

Recently, someone I care deeply about said something very hurtful to me. It was one of those wounds to the deep, sensitive places of my heart. After many tears and much prayer, I had two choices facing me. I could either spend the day in self-pity and spiral into the pit, or climb up on my Daddy's lap. In the past, I might have chosen the pit, but not now. I don't ever want to waste another day in self-pity that I could spend in His presence.

Read Exodus 33. In verses 1-3, what did the Lord tell Moses He was going to do?

_____

_____

As Abba's child, you have the privilege of climbing up on your heavenly Daddy's lap and being wrapped in His embrace. This is a gift of grace.

What was Moses' response (verse 15)? _____

_____

_____

I understand Moses' response. No matter how wonderful the Promised Land or mountaintop sounds, nothing is worth being in a place without the Lord. I would rather be in His presence in the wilderness than without Him in the Promised Land.

When my children were young and I pulled them up on my lap when they were hurt, sick, or sad, as I held them and we rocked, the cares of this world disappeared. Many times, they became so relaxed that they drifted off to sleep in my arms.

As *Abba's* child, you have the privilege of climbing up on your heavenly Daddy's lap and being wrapped in His embrace. This is a gift of grace.

According to Ephesians 5:1, who are we? _____

_____

According to Isaiah 30:1-3, what is our fate when we seek solace elsewhere?

_____

_____

According to Isaiah 57:13, how does that compare to the Lord? _____

_____

_____

Read Psalm 118:8, Psalm 62:5, Matthew 11:28, and 1 John 3:19.

How else would you describe refuge in the Lord? _____

_____

_____

_____

God promises us that we can trust Him to set our hearts at rest even when we are weary and burdened. What keeps us from running to Him first? What are our distractions? Why do we, like the children of Israel in Isaiah 30:1-3, desire to go back to Egypt to look for Pharaoh's protection? Why do we look for worldly solutions? Why do we seek people with whom to share our problems and joys instead of the Lord? When the Lord promises to be big enough to take care of us, why would we rather read a self-help book, watch a talk show about our problem, or discuss it with a friend or counselor instead of first taking it to the Lord? The answer may be found in Mark 6:30-32.

God promises us that we can trust Him to set our hearts at rest even when we are weary and burdened.

What did Jesus ask the disciples to do in order to get rest? _____

_____

_____

Getting alone and still in a quiet place with the Lord resolves the problem and meets our need for rest! However, we usually want the quick fix. We want instant answers, and we don't want to stop what we are doing to find them. How much easier it would be if God would just leave the message of hope and help on our voice mail so we could just check it from our car with our cell phone?

We are busy people with many obligations. But we must take time to be alone and still with the Lord. Our Father God doesn't use band-aids. With Him, there must be self-reflection. When we sit on His lap, His light shines brightly into our hearts and our sin becomes evident.

Many of us would rather ignore the sin than deal with it. Unfortunately, sin never goes away by denial. Dealing with the sin in our lives not only requires self-reflection, but it is something that we must do alone. No one else can do it for us. The Lord bids us, *Come with Me by yourselves to a quiet place and get some rest.* When we go to Him by ourselves, He promises we will get the rest we need.

Our earthly fathers can be stumbling blocks to embracing God as our heavenly Father. If you had a father who was distant, absent, too busy, unsupportive, unapproachable, mean, abusive, or conditional in his love, then you might have a difficult time accepting unconditional love from God.

What is your picture of a father? What do you know from Scripture about the difference in your heavenly Father? _____

_____

_____

How does 2 Corinthians 1:2-4 describe your *Abba*? _____

_____

How does Matthew 9:36 describe Jesus? _____

_____

To have compassion is to link your life with someone else's. It is to feel what they feel, rejoice when they rejoice, and weep when they weep. Compassion is exactly what you will experience on your heavenly Daddy's lap.

There have been times when I have sought help or protection from someone, and it was disastrous. They did not understand, they condemned or judged me, or they were simply powerless to help me.

In Psalm 34:22, what is Father God's promise to us when we seek refuge in Him?

_____

_____

According to Psalm 36:7, why? _____

_____

_____

The Lord bids us, Come with Me by yourselves to a quiet place and get some rest.

To have compassion is to link your life with someone else's. It is to feel what they feel, rejoice when they rejoice, and weep when they weep.

Read Psalm 71:3. Are there ever times when we cannot seek refuge in His arms?

_____

_____

What are the conditions for you to seek Him? _____

_____

According to Psalm 57:1-2 and 61:3-4, is there a time limit for seeking God?

_____

_____

Psalm 17:7 says,

> Show the wonder of your great love, you who save by your right hand
> those who take refuge in you from their foes.

Sometimes you are just hurt. It is not sin in your life. You are the victim. Let your *Abba* show you the wonder of His great love as He holds you in His arms of compassion.

Sometimes you are angry. You have been betrayed. David experienced the same thing in Scripture. What did he do? He sought refuge in the Lord because he knew that was the best and only place to be.

Read 2 Samuel 22:3 and Psalm 7:10. When you need refuge, why should you go to the Lord? _____

_____

_____

The amazing thing about the Lord is that He doesn't just provide a safe place for us to rest; He redeems our hurts, anger, and betrayal. He is our Redeemer for yesterday, today, and tomorrow. The Greek word translated *redeem* is *ga'al*, meaning to redeem, deliver, avenge, or act as a kinsman.[15]

In biblical times, the nearest relative was accountable to redeem their family member out of slavery, financial difficulties, or even marry them if a woman was widowed without children. The responsibilities of this kinsman-redeemer included preserving the integrity, life, property, and family name of his close relative. Jesus is our Kinsman-Redeemer who redeemed us from the bonds of sin. However, it goes

Let your Abba show you the wonder of His great love as He holds you in His arms of compassion.

The amazing thing about the Lord is that He doesn't just provide a safe place for us to rest; He redeems our hurts, anger, and betrayal. He is our Redeemer for yesterday, today, and tomorrow.

further than just salvation. Every time I have a problem with someone and take it to my Father's lap first, He preserves my integrity. Because I then face the problem with His integrity and direction, there is therefore less need for reconciliation in my life.

What is God's promise to us in Isaiah 48:17? _____
_____
_____

Sometimes it is a hurt so deep that there seems no way out. When I go to my Father's lap and give Him this hurt, He doesn't just soothe the pain, He redeems it. He is my Deliverer, my Avenger, and my Redeemer.

When I go to my Father's lap and give Him this hurt, He doesn't just soothe the pain, He redeems it.

What is God's promise to us in Exodus 6:6? _____
_____
_____

When there is no way out, He redeems it. When the situation seems hopeless, He redeems it. When I can't change how someone has hurt me, He redeems my heart attitude and gives me joy and hope. On my Daddy's lap, He changes my heart and the way I handle things or people. He changes my perspective because I see through His eyes and with His heart. This is reconciliation because through this redemption, Jesus is evident in my life, and this touches the lives of everyone around me. Most important, it changes me into His glory and righteousness.

Is there a person or situation that seems hopeless in your life? Climb up on your Daddy's lap and talk to Him about it. Give Him your bondages, and allow Him to be your refuge, rest, compassion, and redemption.

TRUTHS TO EMBRACE

_____
_____
_____
_____
_____
_____

Week 9

UNITY

If asked, my children would say that they love each other because we are a family. Yet the fighting between them portrays a different picture. First John 5:3 says, *This is love for God: to obey his commands.* When asked what was the most important commandment, Jesus replied in Mark 12:30-31: *Love the Lord your God with all your heart and with all your soul and with all your mind and with all your strength. The second is this: "Love your neighbor as yourself." There is no commandment greater than these.*

As a parent, it grieves me when my children argue, and it pleases my heart when they are unified. I really don't even care if they agree, I just want them to get along because I asked them to. I think that our heavenly Father feels the same way about us. This week we will be studying what the scriptures say about unity – with our Father and with others.

DAY 1
And the Two Shall Become One

DAY 2
Hail to the King!

DAY 3
You're Doing It Wrong!

DAY 4
Knit Together – Forever

DAY 5
Embracing Grace

AND THE TWO SHALL BE ONE

On that day you will realize that I am in my Father, and you are in me, and I am in you.

John 14:20

When I married Bruce, my life changed forever. My name changed. My identity changed. My focus changed. I was no longer a single woman, living on my own, making my own decisions. Life was no longer just about me. Now I had to take my husband's needs and desires into consideration. A bathroom that used to be for one was now for two. A bedroom that used to be for one was now for two. Laundry that used to be for one was now for two, although it seemed more like three! As perfect as the union had seemed at the beginning, we have still gone through times of disappointment and a lack of unity, along with times of absolute bliss. What held us together through the years has been our love for each other and our commitment to this union.

Our marriage on earth is just a shadow of our relationship with God as the Bride of Christ.

Read Ephesians 5:22-32. Keeping in mind that we are the church, both individually and collectively, what does this passage have to say about submission to Christ?

_____

_____

Describe the love of Christ for His Bride._____

_____

How would you describe the profound mystery of your relationship with Christ?

_____

_____

Read Deuteronomy 11:13; 11:22; 19:9; 30:16; Joshua 22:5; 23:11; Matthew 22:37; Mark 12:30; and Luke 10:27.

What held us together through the years has been our love for each other and our commitment to this union.

Our marriage on earth is just a shadow of our relationship with God as the Bride of Christ.

What does God command us to do in these verses? _____

_____

_____

Write out John 14:15. _____

_____

What is the result of loving God? _____

_____

_____

As much as I want to be obedient, I can't do it in my own strength, as least not for very long.

In an earlier lesson, we defined *sin* as the ways we don't love God based on 1 John 5:3. John 14:15 says that *if* we love God, then we *will* obey His commands. Too often we focus more on obedience than love, and that is when we cross from grace into legalism. As much as I want to be obedient, I can't do it in my own strength, as least not for very long.

On the other hand, my lack of obedience is simply sin in my life. If I love someone or something more than my Lord, then that is disobedience. If I truly love the Lord with all my heart, soul, mind, and strength, then there is no room for anything else to come before the Lord. When I love Him this way, I come into unity with other believers because there is nothing between us. But how do I begin to love God that way? The truth is that I can't – God does it through grace!

According to 1 Timothy 1:5, what keeps us from having a loving heart? _____

_____

According to 2 Thessalonians 3:5 and Deuteronomy 30:6, how are our hearts changed? _____

_____

_____

This is incredibly good news! I've tried for years to love the Lord the way His Word commanded, and I've always come up short, feeling like I didn't measure up to the "super Christians" at my church. Then I realized that I was going about it backwards! I was focusing on obedience hoping it would lead to love. Instead, I needed to focus on the Lord, and let Him develop love in me by circumcising my heart and revealing my sin, so that I could repent. Then obedience would come, because nothing would be more important to me than God and His will.

What does Joshua 23:11 say about loving the Lord? _____
_____

If I truly love the Lord with all my heart, soul, mind, and strength, then there is no room for anything else to come before the Lord.

It is so easy to slip from grace into legalism. Obedience sounds honorable until you put it before your love for the Lord. The enemy can be very subtle in his ways to skew your focus.

Read 1 John 5:3. When are His commands burdensome? _____
_____
_____

According to these verses, what is the fruit of loving something more than the Lord?

I needed to focus on the Lord, and let Him develop love in me by circumcising my heart and revealing my sin, so that I could repent.

Matthew 23:6 _____

Matthew 23:7 _____

1 John 3:17 _____

According to these verses, what is the fruit of loving the Lord?

Psalm 18:1 _____

Galatians 5:6 _____

1 Peter 1:8 _____

Colossians 2:2 _____

Colossians 3:14 _____

Philippians 2:2 _____

1 John 4:18 _____

2 John 1:6_____

According to Psalm 36:7, what is the value of God's love for you? _____

_____

_____

According to these verses, what do we know about God's love for us?

Psalm 13:5 _____

Psalm 17:7 _____

Psalm 18:11 _____

Psalm 31:7 _____

Psalm 32:10 _____

Psalm 40:11 _____

1 John 4:8 _____

God's love is all-encompassing. I cannot wrap my finite mind around His love, and I will never experience this kind of love anywhere else on earth. His love makes me feel loved, secure, energized, hopeful, encouraged, desired, directed, complete, and safe. There are no voids in my life that His love cannot fill. He gives me His love to experience, return to Him, and give to others. How can that be? I can't explain it – His love is given simply based on His grace alone. In Ephesians 3:17-19, the apostle Paul prayed for us to have an understanding of this love.

We become one with Him as the Bride of Christ and His beloved children.

Let's look at these verses more closely.

Ephesians 3:17-19 says: *And I pray that you, being rooted and established in love, may have power, together with all the saints, to grasp....* The word translated in the Greek here is *katalambano,* meaning to lay hold of so as to make one's own, to take into oneself, or to appropriate.[1]

We need to accept this love and allow God to make it "who we are" so that He can "appropriate" it into our lives. We become one with Him as the Bride of Christ and

His beloved children. This is one true promise that you can hold on to in the joys and trials of life.

- *how wide* – His love is boundless.
- *and long* – His love is endless.
- *and high* – His love is measureless.
- *and deep* – His love is fathomless.

…is the love of Christ, and to know…. The word translated in the Greek here is *ginosko,* which implies that He gives us the capacity to know Him with an intimate know-ledge. This is a term that is a Jewish idiom for sexual intercourse. We can know God with the intimate knowledge reserved for a husband and his bride.[2]

…this love that surpasses knowledge, that you may be filled…. The word translated in the Greek here is *pleroo,* which implies that His love renders us perfect. It completes us so that we are wanting nothing. It accomplishes His purpose in and through us.[3]

…to the measure of all the fullness of God.

This kind of agape love is our identity. It is a sacrificial, costly, permanent, redemptive, unconditional, accepting, affirming, and covenant-keeping love. It is based on God's character and what Jesus did for us on Calvary – not on our beha-vior. It produces in us obedience and a desire to completely align in unity with our Father God.

His love renders us perfect.

What is our promise in John 14:20? _____

_____

_____

Isn't that amazing? We have an intimate knowledge of the Lord because we are one with Him. This, my friend, is unity. We are inseparable because we are part of each other. We become as one in unity with the Lord.

Rewrite John 14:20, inserting your name in the place of the word *you.*

_____

_____

_____

_____

Now read the verse you wrote *out loud*. Repeat it until you believe it. Repeat it every day until it becomes who you believe and know you are.

John 17 records a precious prayer time between Jesus and His Father on the night He was arrested.

What is Jesus' prayer for us in John 17:11, 22? _____

_____

_____

_____

Unity with God means separation from the world, worldly thinking, and worldly actions. It means submission to His will and His ways.

When we are in unity with God, we are under His protection. We are part of Him, and He is part of us. Unity is a decision, an act of the will for each of us, not an emotion. But disunity is an emotion.

According to John 17:13-15, what is the result of unity with the Lord? _____

_____

_____

According to John 17:6, what happens when we are unified with the Lord? _____

_____

_____

When we are in unity with the Father, nothing else matters to us but His will (carried out through our obedience).

Unity with God means separation from the world, worldly thinking, and worldly actions. It means submission to His will and His ways. This submission brings us under His protection and jurisdiction. We are no longer under the standards of the world – what freedom and joy!

What does John 16:12-15 promise? _____

_____

What did Jesus pray in Mark 14:36? Why? _____

_____

Jesus could pray this way because He was in complete unity with His Father. When we are in unity with the Father, nothing else matters to us but His will (carried out through our obedience). We move as one unit under His direction.

The times of controversy in my life have occurred when I stepped away from unity with my Lord to take things into my own hands.

Meditate today on Colossians 3:14. Ask the Lord give you the power to understand the width, length, height, and depth of His love and to appropriate it in your life in unity.

TRUTHS TO EMBRACE

_____

_____

_____

_____

_____

_____

HAIL TO THE KING!

Obey your leaders and submit to their authority. They keep watch over you as men who must give an account. Obey them so that their work will be a joy, not a burden, for that would be of no advantage to you.

Hebrews 13:17

The first Bible study that I led was a neighborhood study at a friend's home. I was very nervous, especially when I saw that several older, godly women from my church as well as several other denominations had shown up. I wanted to turn and run away. Who was *I* to teach *them*?

Instead, I opened the Bible study by having each woman introduce herself. About halfway around the circle, one of those older, godly women spoke up. She said that she was so excited to be at my church because it was growing. Each week she felt like the sermons got better and church grew more exciting.

I was speechless. I had been miserable in our services. In my opinion, our pastor's sermons were dry and totally unprepared. How could this woman be having a completely different worship experience – in the same service?! I took my confusion to the Lord, and He eloquently explained. This woman was coming to church with a heart prepared to worship her Lord. I came wanting to be fed from the sermon and motivated by the service. Her focus was on the Lord; mine was on myself. When I repented and gave my Sunday morning time to the Lord, amazingly, the next week was wonderful! The preaching did not change at all – what changed was *me*!

When my focus is on Jesus, and I come with a heart prepared to worship, the Holy Spirit can speak to me through anyone or anything.

When my focus is on Jesus, and I come with a heart prepared to worship, the Holy Spirit can speak to me through anyone or anything. Many a church has split or members have left because they were dissatisfied with the leadership or did not get what "they wanted" from the service. When this happens, our focus is not on God, but on man.

Up until the time of King Saul, Israel was ruled by judges appointed by God. Israel's focus changed, however, when the last judge, Samuel, was getting old.

Read 1 Samuel 8:5 and 19. Why did the Israelites want a king? _____

_____

_____

When we look for another human being to solve our problems or meet our needs, we have moved our focus away from God.

According to 1 Samuel 8:6-18, what did the Lord warn the Israelites would be the outcome of their focus on an earthly king? _____

_____

_____

Saul was the first king of Israel. What happens to the leadership of the nation of Israel (including Judah) following Saul's reign (2 Sam. 2:10)? _____

_____

_____

When we look for another human being to solve our problems or meet our needs, we have moved our focus away from God. This causes a lack of satisfaction which leads to division, because nothing can satisfy us but the Lord. Even worse is the division and condemnation we face when we try to force others to think and act just like us! Instead of our differences, we need to focus on what we have in common – Jesus.

According to Philippians 3:14-16, what is to be our goal?_____

_____

If we disagree on a situation, to whom should we turn as the revealer of truth?

_____

_____

According to Hebrews 12:1-2, what is to be our focus? _____

_____

According to Hebrews 12:14, what is the result of a lack of holiness in our lives?

_____

_____

Like the Israelites, I had my focus on an "earthly king." When I came to church focused on the pastor, worship leader, or the person sitting behind me, there was no peace in my life, and I missed the Lord and the message He had for me. But when I began to pray for my pastor, God changed my heart. If I had looked elsewhere for another pastor of a different church to be my "king," all I would have done was take my problem to a new location.

According to Isaiah 55:12, how will the Lord lead you to a new church? _____
_____
_____

According to 1 Corinthians 3:10-17, how does God feel about people who destroy His church?_____
_____
_____

When I began to pray for my pastor, God changed my heart.

How does Ephesians 3:6 describe the church? _____
_____

Read Ephesians 2:13-14. Who brings us together in our differences? _____
_____

According to Philippians 2:1-5, what is our call? _____
_____

Describe the church in Acts 4:32. _____
_____
_____

Is there someone in your church with whom you have a problem? It may be an openly stated problem, but more likely it is a secret judgment you harbor against them. You may recognize a sin or something with which you disagree in their life, and it bothers you. How are you handling it? Are you ignoring them, gossiping about them, or praying for them? Many times we make jokes about the way some-one acts and pretend it is all in good fun. As seasoned Christians, we would never "gossip," but the jokes, my friend, are the same and equally as hurtful.

Read Ephesians 5:1-7. What does Scripture have to say about "just joking?"_____
_____
_____

Praying for someone who has hurt me means coming to the place where I pray for the Father's will and not my own.

It is impossible to be angry, judgmental, or in disunity with someone for whom you are earnestly praying. Why? Because Jesus only looks at us through eyes of grace — eyes that accept and never condemn, eyes that know us for who we are and love us unconditionally, eyes that see us as holy and righteous. My love for Him should transcend every desire, aggravation, or hurt, so that my highest goal is to please Him through my love for the saints. Praying for someone who has hurt me means coming to the place where I pray for the Father's will and not my own.

Read Philippians 4:4-7.

When I pray with the eyes of Jesus, what will be evident in my life? _____

_____

_____

In verse 6, the Greek word translated *anxious* is *marimnao,* meaning to be anxious, to be troubled with cares, or to seek to promote one's interest.[4] Therefore, when I am anxious, I am focused on my own cares, trying to get *my* way, for *my* best interest.

When you have an issue with someone in your church, especially someone in leadership, what does God command you to do? _____

_____

_____

If you cannot trust this situation to the Lord to handle, what does this say about your relationship with the Father? _____

_____

_____

According to Hebrews 13:17, how are we commanded to respond to the leadership in our church? _____

_____

_____

Does this only apply when they are leading the way we believe in or interpret scripture? _____

Who gives the account to God for their leadership? _____

_____

During a time of growth, the leadership of our church asked our membership to vote on adding two staff members to accommodate the increased number of programs. The staff had spent much time in prayer about this decision before presenting it to the church. The day of the vote, my Sunday school class was grumbling about the issue when the teacher asked my opinion. I told them that I would vote as my staff requested. I knew they had sought the Lord and that He had given them, not me, the vision for leading our church into the future. By submitting to their leadership, I knew that if they were wrong, God would deal with them, and if they were right, our church would be heading in a new and exciting direction. However, if I refused to submit to their authority, God would deal with my disobedience. I prefer to take the easy way out, and let God have his way with those around me!

I prefer to take the easy way out, and let God have his way with those around me!

Read Daniel 3:13-15. Describe King Nebuchadnezzar and his attitude to God almighty._____

_____

_____

From reading Daniel 4:18-19, how would you describe Daniel's attitude and behavior toward this evil king? _____

_____

_____

Read Daniel 4:36-37. After Daniel submitted to the authority of the king and stayed out of the way while God dealt with King Nebuchadnezzar, what was the outcome?

_____

_____

_____

Once when I had a major disagreement with several staff members, I reacted in the flesh and tried to fix them and the situation instead of submitting to their authority on the issue. The result was disastrous for my family, my church, and myself. My family decided to leave the church in our anger, and we began attending another church. But every time I drove past our old church, I would have a knot in my stomach. I hated to be reminded of this hurt every time I drove down that road!

God impressed upon me that we were a family, and we needed to stay together and work things out. The most important thing in the body of Christ is unity.

More important, it didn't matter who had the correct stand on the issue; by not submitting to my church leadership, I was standing in the way of what God wanted to do in all of our lives. Second Corinthians 6:3 says, *We put no stumbling block in anyone's path, so that our ministry will not be discredited.* When I react in the flesh instead of responding, I put a stumbling block in the path.

My family and I eventually decided to return to our church. God impressed upon me that we were a family, and we needed to stay together and work things out. The most important thing in the body of Christ is unity.

Philippians 1:27 says, *Whatever happens, conduct yourselves in a manner worthy of the gospel of Christ.*

In the light of today's lesson, apply this verse to your life. _____

_____

_____

_____

The most precious gift I received that Christmas was given to me after our Christmas Eve service. A woman came up to me with tears in her eyes. She hugged me and told me how happy she was to see us back at the church. She said that I had witnessed to her by returning because she knew that I had set my own feelings aside to do the will of my Father and glorify Him through my life.

Beloved, life is not about you or me. Our purpose is to do the will of the Lord even when it doesn't make sense, when we are judged incorrectly, when we are hurt, or when it is difficult. God may not resolve the situation as quickly as we'd like or in the exact manner we'd prefer, but He *will* resolve it.

Make a commitment to pray for the leadership in your church on a regular basis. God has placed them in authority for a reason, and He will anoint them and move them in His manner and timing. Remember, they need our prayers and support.

TRUTHS TO EMBRACE

_____

_____

_____

_____

_____

_____

YOU'RE DOING IT WRONG!

Accept one another, then, just as Christ accepted you, in order to bring praise to God.

Romans 15:7

When God convicts someone, the result is true conviction and repentance.

My husband's family always went to Rockport, Texas for their family vacations. Year after year, they left at the same time of the day, ate breakfast at the same restaurant, stayed at the same resort, bought gas in the same town, even fished in the same spot! After we were married, Bruce and I went to Rockport on vacation with his brother and sister. We made reservations at a random resort and decided to leave on Friday after work. Upon hearing our plans, Bruce's father called us and exclaimed, "You're doing it wrong!" Then he proceeded to explain how *they* did it. The truth was that we were not wrong; we were just different in our thinking.

Very often we want others to think and act like us because we want them to validate that we are right.

Read Romans 14:1-6. How are we to respond to people who think differently than we do on issues not specifically addressed by the Word? _____
_____
_____

Read Romans 14:9-13. Who is to act as a judge? Why? _____
_____

According to Romans 14:22, if you differ with someone on a "gray" issue, how should you handle it? _____
_____
_____

When God convicts someone, the result is true conviction and repentance. But when we try to convict or convince someone in our flesh, the result is condemnation. We must extend grace to one another as we have been commanded to do in Romans 15:7: *Accept one another, then, just as Christ accepted you, in order to bring praise to God.*

How does Christ accept us? _____
_____

Very often we want others to think and act like us because we want them to validate that we are right. This legalistic attitude is evidence of our insecurity, instead of our security in the Lord. Max Lucado, in his book, *He Still Moves Stones*, writes, "As long as you think you can control people's behavior toward you, you are held in bondage by their opinions."[5] Instead, we need to be held in the bondage of God's opinion of us.

How does Ephesians 5:1-2 describe the way God looks at us? _____
_____

Read John 4:36-38. Does everyone do the same job? How is this a picture of the body of Christ? _____
_____
_____

There will be unity in the body of Christ when we realize that it takes different gifts and personalities to accomplish God's purposes.

There will be unity in the body of Christ when we realize that it takes different gifts and personalities to accomplish God's purposes. It is time we begin to celebrate our differences and join together in unity with a heart for Jesus.

I am involved in an interdenominational women's ministry called Embracing Grace Ministries. We host a monthly women's Bible study across denominational, ethnic, and racial lines. It has been the joy of my heart to worship God with other women and to study His Word together. Our Bible study hosts women from a variety of races and backgrounds – from Catholic to Protestant to charismatic – yet we all feel the freedom to worship together. We study the Word of God, not any specific church doctrine. The outcome is unity in the body of Christ and the glorification of God.

Philippians 2:1-5 calls us to be "like-minded." Write out your own definition of what you think this passage means to be "like-minded."_____
_____
_____

Read 1 Corinthians 6:1-8. When we argue and disagree, how does God describe us?
_____
_____
_____
_____

According to verse 7, what does this focus on issues without value to the kingdom show about our lives? _____

_____

_____

The emphasis on arguing about our particular beliefs will keep someone from coming to Christ because they see dissension in our life and a lack of unconditional love.

Will anyone be kept out of heaven because they like only hymns or only praise music? What if they don't use a quiet time to start their day? What if they don't believe in all the gifts of the Spirit? What if they do? What about drinking or dancing? These are all issues about which we have our own opinions, convictions, and even scripture references to prove our point; however, if we are wrong, will it affect our salvation? *No!* However, sometimes the emphasis on arguing about our particular beliefs will keep someone from coming to Christ because they see dissension in our life and a lack of unconditional love.

According to verse 6, what is the witness of two Christians who are fighting?

_____

_____

According to 1 Thessalonians 4:11-12, how do we also witness to unbelievers?

_____

_____

According to Galatians 5:14, how are we commanded to love our neighbors?

_____

_____

According to Galatians 5:15, what will happen if we don't? _____

_____

_____

According to Galatians 5:26, what happens when we become conceited or arrogant in our Christian walk? _____

_____

_____

Why would anyone want to be a Christian if all they see is our fighting and arguing? There must be something different about us and something different about the way we handle disagreements. They need to be handled with the grace and love of Jesus Christ.

However, sometimes we come face-to-face with a situation we cannot ignore. We may see a sister in Christ living in sin, and after much prayer, we know that God wants to use us to bring her back onto the narrow path.

Read Galatians 6:1-5. What kind of person is supposed to go to a brother or sister who is caught in sin? _____

_____

_____

The spiritual person knows that except by the grace of God, they could be involved in that same sin.

Read Galatians 5:16-18 and 5:22-23. Write out your own definition of a spiritual person. _____

_____

_____

Galatians 6:1 says, *Brothers, if someone is caught in a sin, you who are spiritual should restore him gently. But watch yourself, or you also may be tempted.* The Greek word translated *gently* is *prautes*. It means with meekness and humility.[6] This is not just outward behavior or a disposition but an inwrought grace of the soul. The spiritual person knows that except by the grace of God, they could be involved in that same sin. They know that apart from God, they are capable of any sin, any depth of depravity. When you restore someone "gently," you are not pointing your finger at them in haughty disapproval. Instead, you are offering them forgiveness and freedom in Christ (Gal. 5:1). Gentle restoration is an integral part of the ministry of reconciliation as you reconcile that believer back to the One who died on their behalf.

When you restore someone "gently," you are not pointing your finger at them in haughty disapproval. Instead, you are offering them forgiveness and freedom in Christ

What do you think the temptation is that is referred to in Galatians 6:1?

_____

_____

_____

We cannot work our way into righteousness.

When we think that we would never have done what someone else did, we are living by the law and not by grace. We cannot work our way into righteousness. James 2:10 says, *For whoever keeps the whole law and yet stumbles at just one point is guilty of breaking all of it.* Our standard is to be God's perfection, not just being better than our neighbor!

How does Jesus describe the:

• Murderer in Matthew 5:21-22? _____

• Adulterer in Matthew 5:27-32? _____

What does Galatians 6:3 say about the person who thinks that he is above reproach?

_____

_____

What are we commanded to do in Galatians 6:2? _____

_____

_____

_____

When you confront someone who is in sin, you do not do it to "catch them." Confronting someone is to be Jesus to them. Jesus never tolerated sin. He called it what it was and told the sinner to repent.

To whom did Jesus come in Matthew 11:28-30? _____

What did He want to do for them? _____

How did Jesus describe Himself?_____

_____

Jesus never asked us to do something that He has not already done Himself. In Matthew 11:28-30 and Galatians 5:1, He modeled what He commands us to do in Galatians 6:1-5. Jesus was tempted and tested by Satan, and when we are used by the Lord to reconcile believers back to His ways, we will be tempted and tested too.

What is the warning given in 1 Peter 5:6-9? _____

_____

_____

A lion is very powerful, controlling, and manipulative. He is the "king of the jungle" and knows how to take advantage of a situation. Satan does the same to us. He will try to blindside you and deceive you. For this reason, don't be surprised if, when you are ministering to a backslidden sinner, you come across the same test in your own life.

I have shared my sin of not submitting to my pastor because I thought he was "doing it wrong." What I didn't tell you was that at that time I was our church's Women's Ministry Coordinator. Several years earlier, before I accepted that position, I had met with my pastor. I told him that if we ever disagreed on some issue, I would submit to his authority because of the scriptural command. I had also stressed this to the other women under my authority. I truly believed that I had this concept down. But when I was tested at the point of my weakness, at a time when I was unguarded, I failed miserably.

Is there someone in your life who you think is "doing it wrong?" Before you confront them, seek the face of God and ask Him to reveal the areas in your own life of which you are prideful and unaware. Then embrace God's grace and extend it to those who are in need of mercy.

> *And the God of all grace, who called you to his eternal glory in Christ, after you have suffered a little while, will himself restore you and make you strong, firm and steadfast. To him be the power for ever and ever. Amen.*
>
> *1 Peter 5:10-11*

When I was tested at the point of my weakness, at a time when I was unguarded, I failed miserably.

```
╔════════════════════════════════════════╗
║         TRUTHS TO EMBRACE                ║
║  _____    ║
║  _____    ║
║  _____    ║
║  _____    ║
║  _____    ║
║  _____    ║
╚════════════════════════════════════════╝
```

Week Nine, Day Four

KNIT TOGETHER—FOREVER

After David had finished talking with Saul, Jonathan became one in spirit with David, and he loved him as himself.

1 Samuel 18:1

The Bible portrays friendship as a special and sacred covenant relationship.

One of my favorite movies is *Steel Magnolias*. I love the way the women in that movie stick together through good times and bad. They are all very different, but all of them love and care for each other. Today, one of the popular things to do among pre-teen and teenage girls is to exchange "best friend" necklaces. One friend wears a necklace with half a heart, and the other friend wears the other side. The necklaces symbolize their friendship. Little boys, on the other hand, used to show their loyalty to each other by becoming "blood brothers." They would each cut themselves, place their cuts together until their blood mixed, and thus become a part of each other forever. As adults today, these rituals may seem silly, but I believe there is great biblical truth in them for unity in our friendships. The Bible portrays friendship as a special and sacred covenant relationship. Unlike the relationships in our family, these are relationships which we choose, and they should be relationships in which we are of one heart and one mind.

How does Proverbs 17:17 describe a friend? _____

_____

_____

After we moved to Tomball and my children were to attend a new school, my youngest son Brad came home after the first day. I asked Brad with whom he had eaten lunch since he didn't know anyone. He smiled and said, "I ate with my friend, Shane, and my friend, Michael." Now, Brad had just met those boys that day, and he already considered them to be his friends. In reality, we need to choose our friends a little more wisely. These boys were actually acquaintances who might become friends later.

Jesus had twelve close friends. Of these twelve, there was one who would betray Him, three to whom He was closest, and one who was referred to as the "one He loved." We need to distinguish our close friends. A few weeks ago, I asked you to determine your twelve closest friends.

Who are the three in your inner circle to whom you are the closest? Who is the one that you love best? _____

_____

In John 13:23, how does John refer to himself?_____

_____

How close was he to Jesus at dinner? _____

_____

When you are with a group of people, who are the friends next to whom you usually sit?_____

_____

John was in Jesus' inner circle along with Peter and James.

Read John 18:15-16.

It is believed that the "other disciple" in this passage is John.

Who was the first to arrive at Jesus' trial and the only one who stayed while Jesus was questioned by Annas? _____

Read John 20:1-9. Who were the first two disciples to arrive at the tomb? _____

_____

_____

Read John 19:25-27. Who was the only disciple mentioned at the crucifixion?

_____

What would lead you to believe that, on earth, Jesus considered John His closest and most trusted friend? _____

_____

What does Proverbs 18:24 mean to you? _____

_____

_____

_____

It is important to discern our friends, our closer friends, and our best friends because those roles fill different relationship needs in our life. When we confuse these roles or have expectations of a casual friend filling our need for a close and trusted friend, we risk disappointment. This study is about reconciliation, and there is a great need for that in our relationships with friends and acquaintances. Remember, even our best friends will sometimes let us down, and they cannot and should never fill the space reserved for our Lord and Savior.

Read Mark 14:32-42.

Jesus needed support as He prayed to His Father before He was arrested, tried, beaten, and sentenced to be killed. To whom did He turn at this time? _____

_____

Did His friends let Him down? How? _____

_____

According to Luke 22:43, where did He find strength? _____

_____

Have you ever had a friend let you down when you specifically asked for their help? Describe the situation. _____

_____

_____

To whom were you looking for strength? _____

_____

_____

Read Matthew 26:31-35 and Mark 14:27-31. What did Peter promise Jesus? Do you think he meant what he said at the time? _____

_____

_____

Remember, even our best friends will sometimes let us down, and they cannot and should never fill the space reserved for our Lord and Savior.

According to Luke 22:54-62, what did Peter do when push came to shove?_____

_____

_____

How did Jesus respond to Peter? _____

_____

_____

I think that when Jesus looked at Peter, He looked at him with eyes full of love, compassion, grace, and forgiveness. That is why Peter wept so bitterly. He saw that even though he turned his back on his friend and his Lord, Jesus' feelings for Peter remained unchanged. Theirs was a covenant relationship based on Jesus' love, not Peter's actions. What are your expectations for your friends? Are they based on love and grace, or works?

When Jesus looked at Peter, He looked at him with eyes full of love, compassion, grace, and forgiveness.

Although we are talking about the kind of friends we need, we also need to learn what kind of friend we should be ourselves, based on God's Word.

Read 1 Samuel 18:1-4, and chapters 19 and 20. Describe the covenant relationship between David and Jonathan. _____

_____

_____

_____

In the *King James Version* of 1 Samuel 18:1, it says that their souls were "knit together" – forever. The covenant relationship between these two young men was strong because God had knit their souls together in unity.

Read Ecclesiastes 4:9-12. Who is the third strand in our covenant friendships?__

_____

_____

What can one friend do when the other one falls down? _____

_____

What are ways that you have helped your friends up when they fell down? _____

_____

_____

One of the reasons we need to choose our friends wisely is that they are there to help us when we are down. We need friends who encourage us to walk in God's ways even when it is hard. They hold us accountable and discern God's truth and wisdom when we can't or won't on our own. But just as important, we need to be that kind of friend to others. We need to be sure that when we're offering help or advice, we are doing it "in Christ Jesus," not in our own strength.

We need friends who encourage us to walk in God's ways even when it is hard.

According to 1 Samuel 23:15-16, when David was in exile and running from Saul in fear for his life, how did Jonathan help him? _____

_____

_____

_____

Jonathan was Saul's son and privy to a great deal of confidential information. It would have been very easy for him to take matters into his own hands and form his own plan to help David, but instead he trusted in God and His Word.

Read 1 Corinthians 15:33.

In today's society, we talk a lot about compromise, but God's Word is black and white.

The word *misled* is translated from the Greek word, *planao,* which means to cause to wander, to lead astray, to deceive, or to cause to form a wrong judgment.[7] A person may not be a good choice for a close friend, not necessarily because they are an evil person. They may just cause us to water down our faith or walk too closely to the line. In today's society, we talk a lot about compromise, but God's Word is black and white. We cannot allow compromise to invade our walk with Christ.

Have you ever had a friend that subtly caused you to compromise your faith? If so, what happened? _____

_____

_____

Second Corinthians 6:14 commands us not to be_____

_____

_____.

Does this mean that we should never have unbelieving friends? No, in fact many times that is how we witness to unbelievers. However, our *closest* friends should be believers or we will never be in complete unity. Close friends exert a great deal of influence on our life, and vice versa. These should be relationships that draw both parties closer to the Lord.

I have been so fortunate in my life. God has brought me several godly women to be my close friends. They have mentored me, ministered to me, spoke truth to me when I needed it, and drawn me closer to Christ. I honestly cannot imagine my spiritual life without them. Although we have not always agreed on everything, we have always been in unity in our faith and love, and that has been enough.

If a special friend (or friends) has not come into your life, you still have the best Friend of all.

According to John 15:13-17, who is your Friend? _____

_____

_____

He has chosen you, loves you unconditionally, and has laid down His life for you. He is available anytime you call, and He will never abandon you. He will correct you when you are wrong, and encourage you when you are on the right track. He will never betray you. He is your best Friend, and your hearts are knit together – forever.

Close friends exert a great deal of influence on our life, and vice versa.

TRUTHS TO EMBRACE

_____

_____

_____

_____

_____

EMBRACING GRACE

All this is from God, who reconciled us to himself through Christ and gave us the ministry of reconciliation.

2 Corinthians 5:18

Embracing grace is being totally enthralled with the God who loves us right where we are, in the midst of our sin.

I once attended a church that experienced an incredible move of God. Families and individuals were healed, spiritual renewal and growth was taking place, and lives were changed forever. This amazing move of God went on for quite some time. I could hardly wait for the next Sunday or Wednesday service or the next Bible study to see what God would do next. Many of our hearts were bonded together through Jesus Christ forever. We had been to the mountaintop together and seen the Lord. But suddenly everything seemed to slip away. I prayed and pondered what had happened. I loved the Lord so much and was in awe of what He was doing in my life and the lives of those around me. What had happened? When did we start "playing church" again? You see, *we had become more in love with the movement of God than God Himself.*

> *Careful! I've put a huge stone on the road to Mount Zion, a stone you can't get around. But the stone is me! If you're looking for me, you'll find me on the way, not in the way.*
>
> *Romans 9:30-32* THE MESSAGE

Embracing grace is being totally enthralled with the God who loves us right where we are, in the midst of our sin, knowing exactly where we have been and what we have done. It is knowing that left to our own devices we will never be any better. Grace is something that you can't keep to yourself; you must extend it to others.

Read Luke 17:11-19. How is Jesus referred to in verse 13? _____

_____

_____

_____

In our prayer time we often come to our Father with our list of things that we want Him to do. Many of these are noble concerns for the healing of others, but the question is still, "Where is our heart?" Do we go to our Lord just to ask for things? We were created to fellowship with Him, and this should be our first priority. Scripture does instruct us to pray for each other and to intercede on behalf of our brothers and sisters in Christ; however, this needs to be secondary to our relationship with the Father.

What does Luke 17:14 teach us about the free gift of salvation that Jesus offers? Explain. _____

_____

_____

_____

_____

In Luke 17:15-19, isn't it incredible that only one of the men came back to thank Jesus? Yet that is exactly what Romans 9:30-32 demonstrates – that one man actually embraced what God was doing as He straightened out their lives, and the other nine missed it! Why? Because they were only interested in having their leprosy healed (or seeing the movement of God). They were so absorbed in themselves that they missed a life-changing encounter with Jesus. They were looking for a Savior – not the Lord.

They were so absorbed in themselves that they missed a life-changing encounter with Jesus.

The one man who was healed inside and out was never the same. In fact, verse 19 says that he wasn't just healed, he was healed *by faith*. Jesus can heal anyone. The difference with the one man who returned to thank Jesus for his healing is that he was not only saved from leprosy, Jesus was then the Lord of his life. Jesus, not the healing, was his focus.

I have a dear friend who loves to call me after her weekly Bible study and share with me the amazing movement of God that she and others had just experienced. Sadly, in the daily walk of her life, there is no change, no joy, no peace, no evidence of grace. Her walk with the Lord seems to be based solely on these weekly experiences.

Read Luke 5:12-13.

How did the leper approach Jesus? _____

What did Jesus do before He healed the leper? _____
_____

Jesus touches the

untouchable.

Have you ever felt like you were too sick, too dirty, too repulsive, or too deep in sin to look into the eyes of Jesus? If so, when? _____
_____

What was Jesus' response to you at that time? _____
_____
_____

Jesus' willingness to reach

out to us and grab our

hands – no matter what

state we are in – is

amazing.

How do you think others would have responded to you if they knew the truth?
_____
_____
_____
_____

Jesus touches the untouchable. Leprosy at that time was contagious. Lepers were quarantined and never, ever touched again. What an incredibly lonely and hurtful existence! Yet Jesus touched the leper – *before* he was healed of leprosy. Jesus' willingness to reach out to us and grab our hands – no matter what state we are in – is amazing. He is never repulsed by us. Jesus could have just healed the leper, but His touch showed the love and grace of God.

One of the hardest things for me in writing this Bible study has been the exposure of my scars. All the wrong choices, hurts, and sin in my life have affected not just me, but those around me. I have sat at Jesus' feet and pleaded, *Why can't I just write about what I have observed in other people's lives? This is so embarrassing!* But there is no real embarrassment in grace. The embarrassment comes from my pride, my not wanting the scars to show. The truth is that I have experienced God's grace *through* my scars. That is when I truly came to know Him and experienced His love.

I have prayed so many times, *I want to be just like You, Jesus.* But the reality is that Jesus' body was beaten, torn, and full of scars. His very heart was broken as the Father turned away from Him at the cross because of my sin.

One amazing thing about the human body is that when wounded, the resulting scar tissue becomes stronger than the original tissue. The same holds true for the scars in my life. When Jesus heals my wounds, I grow stronger in my walk of grace with Him. We need to celebrate our scars and be willing, like Jesus, to touch the wounds of those around us as we reach out in love, grace, and reconciliation.

Read 2 Corinthians 5:14-21 and put verse 15 into your own words. _____
_____
_____
_____
_____

When Jesus heals my wounds, I grow stronger in my walk of grace with Him.

In 1492, a bitter and bloody feud raged in Ireland. It was between Lord Ormond and Lord Kildare. Lord Ormond and his band sought refuge in the Chapter House. It seemed as if there was no hope of an end to the fighting. Lord Kildare eventually came to Lord Ormond and offered a truce, but they did not trust each other. Lord Kildare finally hacked a hole in the door and reached his hand through to touch the hand of his enemy. This was a huge risk because his arm could have been cut right off! But instead, because someone took the first step, there was reconciliation between these two households. This door is now on display at St. Patrick's Cathedral in Dublin, Ireland; it is a symbol of peace and reconciliation worldwide.

As ministers of reconciliation, God has called us to "thrust our hands through the door" and touch our enemies.

As ministers of reconciliation, God has called us to "thrust our hands through the door" and touch our enemies.

Read John 8:14-18.

From where did you come? _____

Where are you going? _____

Who is with you? _____

Knowing where you have come from and that you can only go forward with Jesus is the first step to embracing grace. Embracing grace means receiving and reaching out with the same graceful touch and unconditional love that Jesus has extended to us.

Knowing where you have come from and that you can only go forward with Jesus is the first step to embracing grace.

We have spent the last nine weeks studying the ministry of reconciliation. It is my prayer that this has been as life changing for you as it has been for me. Before you close this book and set it aside, please take a few moments to write out your own definition of what "Embracing Grace" means, and thank our Lord and Savior, Christ Jesus, for making it possible.

The grace of the Lord Jesus be with God's people. Amen.

Revelation 22:21

TRUTHS TO EMBRACE

_____

_____

_____

_____

_____

_____

END NOTES

Week One

[1] James Strong, *Strong's Greek Dictionary of the New Testament*, #1325.

[2] Oswald Chambers, *My Utmost for His Highest*
  (Grand Rapids: Discovery House, 1992).

[3] James Strong, *Strong's Hebrew and Chaldee Dictionary*, #6887.

[4] Ibid., #5358.

[5] Ibid., #5797.

[6] Strong, *Greek Dictionary*, #2756.

[7] Ibid., #5293.

[8] Ibid., #1210.

Week Two

[1] Strong, *Greek Dictionary*, #3954.

[2] Ibid., #2147.

[3] Strong, *Hebrew Dictionary*, #7065.

[4] Nathan Stone, *Names of God*.

[5] Strong, *Hebrew Dictionary*, #4900.

[6] Ibid., #3820.

[7] Ibid., #2470.

[8] Ibid., #8378.

Week Three

[1] *Webster's New World College Dictionary*, 3rd edition.
  (New York: Simon & Schuster, 1988), "justify."

[2] *Vine's Expository Dictionary*, "justify."

[3] Ibid., "mercy."

[4] Erwin Lutzer, *Overcoming the Grasshopper Complex*
  (Colorado Springs: Chariot Victor, 1991).

[5] Strong, *Greek Dictionary*, #3162.

[6] Ibid., #906.

[7] Ibid., #4198.

[8] Ibid., #4698.

Week Four

[1] Strong, *Greek Dictionary*, #3136.

[2] Ibid., #3686.

[3] Ibid., #2821.

[4] Ibid., #863.

[5] Ibid., #2744.

[6] Ibid., #3628.

[7] Ibid., #5544.

[8] Ibid., #5012.

[9] Ibid., #4236.

[10] Ibid., #3115.

[11] Ibid., #5056.

[12] Ibid., #3107.

[13] Ibid., #25.

[14] Ibid., #906.

[15] Ibid., #5046.

[16] Strong, *Hebrew Dictionary*, #5869.

[17] Ibid., #2620.

[18] Ibid., #5315.

[19] Strong, *Greek Dictionary*, #906.

[20] Ibid., #5319.

[21] Ibid., #870.

[22] Ibid., #5156.

Week Five

[1] Strong, *Greek Dictionary*, #2786.

[2] Ibid., #1223.

[3] Ibid., #3050.

[4] Ibid.

[5] Ibid., #342.

[6] Ibid., #3563.

[7] Ibid., #3309.

[8] Ibid., #5432.

[9] Ibid., #2564.

Week Six

[1] Strong, *Hebrew Dictionary*, #6419.

[2] Strong, *Greek Dictionary*, #5009.

[3] Ibid., #2808.

[4] Ibid., #1342.

[5] Strong, *Hebrew Dictionary*, #1288.

[6] Strong, *Greek Dictionary*, #575.

[7] Ibid., #74.

[8] Ibid., #25.

[9] Strong, *Hebrew Dictionary*, #6419.

Week Seven

[1] Joyce Meyer, *Managing Your Emotions* (Tulsa: Harrison House, 1996).

[2] *Webster's*, "expectation."

[3] Strong, *Greek Dictionary*, #25.

[4] Meyer.

[5] Strong, *Greek Dictionary*, #1722.

[6] Ruth Vaughn and Anita Higman, *Who Will I Be for the Rest of My Life?* (Minneapolis: Bethany House, 1998).

[7] Larry Crabb, *Connecting* (Dallas: Word, 1997).

[8] Strong, *Hebrew Dictionary*, #4196.

Week Eight

[1] Strong, *Greek Dictionary*, #2192.

[2] Ibid., #4100.

[3] Ibid.

[4] Ibid., #3708.

[5] *Webster's*, "sovereign."

[6] Stone.

[7] Ibid.

[8] Strong, *Hebrew Dictionary*, #2803.

[9] Ibid., #7227.

[10] Ibid., #2421.

[11] *Webster's*, "sufficient."

[12] Strong, *Hebrew Dictionary*, #3824.

[13] Ibid., #6381.

[14] *Webster's*, "deliver."

Week Nine

[1] Strong, *Greek Dictionary*, #2638.

[2] Ibid., #1097.

[3] Ibid., #4137.

[4] Ibid., #3309.

[5] Max Lucado, *He Still Moves Stones* (Dallas: Word, 1999).

[6] Strong, *Greek Dictionary*, #4236.

[7] Ibid., #4105.

NOTES

Real Problems... Real People... Real Life... Real Answers...
THE INDISPUTABLE POWER OF BIBLE STUDIES

Through the Bible in One Year
Alan B. Stringfellow • ISBN 1-56322-014-8

God's Great & Precious Promises
Connie Witter • ISBN 1-56322-063-6

Preparing for Marriage God's Way
Wayne Mack • ISBN 1-56322-019-9

Becoming the Noble Woman
Anita Young • ISBN 1-56322-020-2

Women in the Bible — Examples To Live By
Sylvia Charles • ISBN 1-56322-021-0

Pathways to Spiritual Understanding
Richard Powers • ISBN 1-56322-023-7

Christian Discipleship
Steven Collins • ISBN 1-56322-022-9

Couples in the Bible — Examples To Live By
Sylvia Charles • ISBN 1-56322-062-8

Men in the Bible — Examples To Live By
Don Charles • ISBN 1-56322-067-9

7 Steps to Bible Skills
Dorothy Hellstern • ISBN 1-56322-029-6

Great Characters of the Bible
Alan B. Stringfellow • ISBN 1-56322-046-6

Great Truths of the Bible
Alan B. Stringfellow • ISBN 1-56322-047-4

The Trust
Steve Roll • ISBN 1-56322-075-X

Because of Jesus
Connie Witter • ISBN 1-56322-077-6

The Quest
Dorothy Hellstern • ISBN 1-56322-078-4

God's Solutions to Life's Problems
Wayne Mack & Joshua Mack • ISBN 1-56322-079-2

A Hard Choice
Dr. Jesús Cruz Correa • Dr. Doris Colón Santiago
ISBN 1-56322-080-6

11 Reasons Families Succeed
Richard & Rita Tate • ISBN 1-56322-081-4

The Fear Factor
Wayne Mack & Joshua Mack • ISBN 1-56322-082-2

Embracing Grace
Judy Baker • ISBN 1-56322-083-0

Problemas Reales... Gente Real... Vida Real... Respuestas Reales...
EL INDISCUTIBLE IMPACTO DE LOS ESTUDIOS BÍBLICOS

A través de la biblia en un año
Alan B. Stringfellow • ISBN 1-56322-061-X

Preparando el matrimonio en el camino de Dios
Wayne Mack • ISBN 1-56322-066-0

Mujeres en la Biblia
Sylvia Charles • ISBN 1-56322-072-5

Parejas en la Biblia
Sylvia Charles • ISBN 1-56322-073-3

Decisión Difícil
Dr. Jesús Cruz Correa & Dra. Doris Colón Santiago •
ISBN 1-56322-074-1